LIFE CYCLES

Other titles by Bill Anderton:
Inner Alchemy

Bill Anderton, BSc, has developed his interest in the field of transpersonal psychology, and its application to personal growth and human potential. This has led him to work with many individuals, exploring the inner worlds through dreams, active imagination and the symbols of alchemy and astrology. He has presented lectures and workshops on these subjects. Now the commissioning editor for Quantum books, he lives with his family in Gloucestershire.

The computer-generated cover illustration is inspired by a seventeenth century alchemical riddle, 'All things do live in the three/But in the four they merry be,' squaring the circle to make the two sexes one whole (after Jamsthaler, *Viatorium spagyricum*).

LIFE CYCLES

The Astrology of Inner Space &
Its Application to the Rhythms of Life

Bill Anderton

quantum

LONDON • NEW YORK • TORONTO • SYDNEY

quantum

An imprint of W. Foulsham & Co. Ltd., Yeovil Road,
Slough, Berkshire SL1 4JH

ISBN 0–572–01535–6
Copyright © 1990 Bill Anderton

Printed in Great Britain at St Edmundsbury Press, Bury St Edmunds.

Round and round the circle
Completing the charm
So the knot be unknotted
The crossed be uncrossed
The crooked be made straight
And the curse be ended.

T.S. Eliot

CONTENTS

PREFACE

This book is a guide to the cycles, phases and patterns of life that everyone experiences. It shows how cycles are repeated if lessons are not learned or experience gained, how there are crisis points in life to watch out for and work through, and how the basic patterns of life and growth to maturity are described by the symbols of astrology.

Astrology works on the basis of cycles and patterns and these can be related to everyday life. I describe the cycles of the planets, the sun–moon cycle (phases of the moon), the sun's cycle through the zodiac, and the astrological houses, which represent areas of experience connected with the 12 phases of life.

Most people's view of the passage of time is that of a linear flow from past to future, progressing in a manner that is completely independent of the events that occur during its course. There is another view which has always been held by Eastern mystics and is now also subscribed to by the new physics. This view emphasises the interconnectedness of all things, and life is looked upon not as a simple progression of unrelated events but as a process having a recognisable pattern of probable occurrences.

This process is encapsulated in the symbols of astrology. These can reveal the patterns of life that largely go unrecognised because of a failure to see any connection between ourselves and the events that occur during the passage of time. *Life Cycles* will show how that connection can be made, while exploring new dimensions of reality.

These new dimensions are the paradigm for a New Age, the beginnings of whose culture are with us now – environmental awareness, concern for the quality of life, holistic approaches to health and the mind–body relationship. The accepted view of reality is gradually changing as the discoveries of the new physics are made known, and there is the realisation that we cannot hope to understand our world without an understanding of ourselves – our drives, needs, hopes, fears and potential. The giant leaps made by science and technology have not been matched by progress in knowledge and awareness about our own natures. The time is now ripe to achieve such an understanding.

This small book has been several years in gestation, and I do not claim that all of the ideas it contains are original. Indeed, if the reader wishes to pursue further any of the basic ideas presented, there is ample literature to choose from (see pages 153–4).

Readers new to the idea of exploring the inner worlds may find it somewhat bizarre at first. Nevertheless it is to these readers in particular that this book is dedicated. If you are a newcomer to this subject, and the inner path appeals, then I hope to have started you on a way which will lead to inner growth and fulfilment.

Bill Anderton

CHAPTER 1
CYCLES, NOT STRAIGHT LINES

It is generally assumed that time is linear, and moves in a straight line from birth to death. There is a rather different view, however, which is that the time process is one of cyclic change and of unfolding pattern. A few moments' reflection may reveal personal experiences that repeat and relationships that tend to have the same patterns and problems. Have you ever had the feeling of going round in circles? The first step in breaking out of a repeating pattern is to recognise that it exists.

According to virtually all of the different schools of occult and religious thought, mankind has reached a critical point in time in the history of evolution. As we move towards the end of the twentieth century, a new mood is emerging which to a great extent stems from the drastic environmental changes that have taken place throughout this century. These changes have largely been brought about by a predominantly scientific and technological approach to the way we relate to and attempt to mould our environment. The outer changes seem to be precipitating an inner revolution of consciousness. This is probably taking place on a global scale, with varying degrees of conscious awareness in different persons. One can also say that the way an individual relates to the environment may be seen as a reflection of his or her inner processes.

A shift in the way we view ourselves and the world in

which we live is taking place. The change is to some extent a reaction against the prevailing one-sided view of the nature of reality. In modern times so much emphasis has been placed on objectivity and rationalism that human values, the subjective, individualised nature of the imagination and the numinous nature of life itself are insufficiently appreciated. The reaction is manifest in what have been loosely termed 'New Age' activities. These promote individual human values and the idea that human beings, whatever their colour or creed, are members of a global family, the unifying factor being human consciousness. The emphasis is on global awareness, which is facilitated by communications technology, and this awareness is not only of the relationship between all peoples but of that between ourselves and the living planet which we inhabit.

In terms of the history of consciousness, the human race is about to leave adolescence and enter the early years of maturity. There is, however, no growth without pain, and the struggles and difficulties of coping with the problems of modern life are too apparent. One only has to pick up a newspaper to discover the current problems in every area of human activity, from prisons to hospitals, from strikes to inflation, from wars to the limitation of human rights. These represent the pain and suffering that must be dealt with, if we are to move on to the next phase of human evolution.

Intuitively, many people realise this, and are seeking to find ways in which they as individuals can help and take part in this process of growth and healing of our planet. The search is on for new modes of self-expression which are needed to communicate the never-before-faced experiences that are welling up from the inner dimensions of every individual. The name often given to these inner, unknown dimensions is the 'subconscious' – or the 'unconscious', to use the word favoured by the influential Swiss psychologist, Dr Carl Jung. His contention was that the word 'subconscious' implied a sort of psychic dustbin, containing all the unwanted, repressed, negative experiences of the individ-

12

ual. Jung gave his word 'unconscious' a much wider definition than that of the psychic dustbin. The unconscious contains not only elements that are personal to the individual but also includes much that is common to all people. This Jung described as the 'collective unconscious', and its implication is that within every individual lies the potential for experiences that are rooted not in the personal life but in the historic life of the human race. It is the experience of this dimension that we are being called upon to face and acknowledge in the search for expanded awareness with consequent positive effects on the environment, the world in which we live. A further implication of this is that the drama of the unfoldment of our own lives as individuals contains a pattern that is universal in nature – we may feel that 'nothing like this has ever happened to anyone else before', but it has, whether this be to do with personal relationships or mystical experiences.

In Jung's own words[1] —

> A more or less superficial layer of the unconscious is
> undoubtedly personal. I call it the *personal unconscious*. But this
> personal unconscious rests upon a deeper layer, which does not
> derive from personal experience and is not a personal acquisition
> but is inborn. This deeper layer I call the *collective unconscious*. I
> have chosen the term 'collective' because this part of the
> unconscious is not individual but universal; in contrast to the
> personal psyche, it has contents and modes of behaviour that
> are more or less the same everywhere and in all individuals. It
> is, in other words, identical in all men and thus constitutes a
> common psychic substrate of a suprapersonal nature which is
> present in every one of us.

The unconscious does not discriminate – anyone can be taken up by its promptings and swept along on the tide of this New Age.

---

1.   Prof. C.G. Jung, *Four Archetypes – Mother, Rebirth, Spirit, Trickster,* Routledge & Kegan Paul, extracted from Vol. 9, Part 1 of *The Collected Works of C.G. Jung.* The concept of archetypes and its correlate, that of the collective unconscious, are among the best known theories introduced by Jung. Volume 9 of *The Collected Works* consists of writings describing and elaborating the two concepts.

The ordinary person naturally finds it hard to know what he or she can do to help, in the face of power politics, or the commercial giants, or the sheer immensity of the task that must be faced in solving even the smallest of the world's many problems. But this dilemma of the individual was the prime reason for my writing this book.

I believe that the most important factor in shaping life on our planet is the individual. I am *for* the individual because in each and every one of us shines a living star, the light of consciousness. We are each our own universe. It is the nature of the individual inner universe that this book seeks to explore in a manner which I hope will show how everyone can follow this path of discovery. It is possible that this may be one way in which we can achieve the next stage of our evolution, of the maturing of consciousness. If we remain in ignorance of the inner processes that take place within the psyche, these will then be externalised and appear reflected in the world that we view around us. So our own inner tensions are seen as strife and suffering in our personal relationships and the world at large. Therefore, because only the symptoms are revealed and not the root causes, it is not possible to deal with the real cause of the world's pain that lies within the nature of individual human consciousness.

In an article published in the journal *Soluna*, Anne Baring wrote —

> The unconscious is perhaps the most important discovery of this century. Yet it is extraordinary that with the exception of a few men and women, the concept that our nature is dual and consists of both conscious and unconscious aspects is not generally understood, let alone applied to our lives. There is available to us an immense treasure of insight into and understanding of the psyche that could lead us out of the labyrinth where at present we are wandering without any helpful ball of string . . .
>
> Let us turn for a moment to the conditions of the outer world. We are worried by many things: inflation, unemployment, the population explosion, the growth of the power of the state, the threat of further blood-baths in Africa and the Middle East, the

fear of Soviet military power. Above all, perhaps, we are alarmed by the growth of anarchy and terrorism and the eruption of every kind of cruelty, depravity and violence. We try to deal with these various symptoms of some profound process of change that our civilisation is undergoing. Our attention, however, is rigidly fixed on the external world which is the only one we take account of. It is so far impossible for us to entertain the hypothesis that every one of these colossal problems is the outcome, the reflection, of what takes place in the invisible and unknown world of the psyche and that it is the inner world that creates the conditions of the outer one . . .

Looking at the terrible conflicts, choices and dangers which surround us on every side, it is not hard to come to the conclusion that the principle thing that is wrong with the world is man. The greatest danger comes from our almost total ignorance of how our nature works and how we are controlled by the instinctive patterns of behaviour that arise from the collective unconscious within us.

For the individual, this lack of inner awareness can result in paranoia, the sensation of being followed, of being got at, of persecution, of secret plotting. A woman whom I met some time ago described how, whenever she started a new job, there was always at least one man who fell in love with her. She never confronted the particular person who would remain completely ignorant of this allegation. The woman in question told endless stories of being followed and pestered, when in fact the amorous intentions were a complete figment of her imagination. In fact, she was being 'chased' by impulses and feelings that stemmed from inside herself rather than having anything to do with the unsuspecting man. Every time, rather than confronting her feelings, the woman would get in such a state that eventually she would leave her job, saying that the unwanted attention of her supposed suitor was too much to bear. At the next job, the same situation would arise and the whole pattern of events would be repeated.

This is an extreme case, perhaps, but every day we are all haunted by the ghosts of our inner life that come at us from the outside world; the events that occur, our successes and failures, the way our relationships turn out, the things people say and do, are all partly in response to our inner selves, whether or not we are aware of this.

Collective paranoia can be seen at work in conflicting political views, where one country is always cast as the villain, such as the modern Western world's attitude to communism and the Eastern bloc. The real threat rarely lies 'out there' in the stereotyped image of bad people or a bad country, but comes from within the human psyche, with its unresolved, unconscious conflicts, giving rise to a negative outer expression. The path to solving the world's problems is not just a matter of political endeavour – an inner awareness is needed.

For the individual, the way is wide open. You don't need a bottomless purse to embark upon this expedition into the unknown, or need to wait for the right weather conditions, or the right angle of the earth's inclination to Jupiter, before you can blast off! All that is needed is the will to explore one's own inner nature.

As soon as this journey of self-exploration and discovery is embarked upon, it becomes apparent that a line of communication is being opened up between the conscious ego and the inner processes which are functioning on an unconscious level. Everyday awareness of ourselves (self-consciousness = the 'ego') represents only a small part of the field of consciousness. At any one time, it is only possible to be partially aware. We can call things into consciousness temporarily – memories, ideas, thoughts, day-dreams, feelings, sensations – but they are soon replaced by other fragments of awareness. This can give an idea of the sum total of the *possible* contents of consciousness – just think what it would be like to remember every single personal experience simultaneously – and shows how small the actual field of awareness really is. Even when we are not aware of all the possible contents of consciousness, these continue to 'live' within us and remain as part of the personal unconscious until called upon. Even though they are unconscious, these aspects of the personality continue to affect and even control our daily lives, our responses to situations and to people.

There are contents of the unconscious which lie at such a deep level that we rarely experience them directly. These are called 'archetypes' and influence the basic patterns of not only our own lives but those of every person in the society in which we live. They are representatives of the collective unconscious and can be described as the underlying patterns that lie behind all of our daily experiences. Religions, both ancient and modern, mythologies and esoteric systems, such as astrology and the tarot, provide us with descriptions of the archetypes of the unconscious. They are portrayed as gods, stereotypes, or particular qualities such as 'justice', or 'rebirth', which themselves are often personified. For each archetype there is an associated image which is usually represented as a certain type of man or woman. Thus we have the archetypal image of death, represented in astrology and in Roman mythology by the personality of Saturn. We have the archetypal image of love, represented by Venus, and so on. It is important to differentiate between the image of the archetype and the archetype itself. The archetype always remains hidden to us. The archetypal image helps us to understand the archetype by clothing it in a particular way, giving us something to experience directly. The archetypal image gives the archetype content.

The archetypes are the blueprint on which our behaviour patterns are built. Our own life patterns may superficially appear to be unique, personal happenings, but the underlying archetypes, the driving forces, are elements common to human nature. Learn about Venus and much will be revealed about the nature of love; learn about Saturn and a door is opened into the mysteries of death.

The term 'archetype' was not coined in modern times and can be found in classical literature, but it has become part of the terminology of modern psychology, although its historic reference to the *Imago Dei*, the God-image in man, is apt.

The unconscious can never be entered into directly, for to do so would mean that the individual becomes unconscious. Somehow, its content must come to us, or at least a line of communication must be established, and one way to do this can be through the creative use of the imagination. In other words, the imagination may be used to create a meaningful link between the conscious and the unconscious self.

I use the word 'imagination' advisedly here, because one person's imagination is another's reality, and vice versa. The experiences of the religious mystic may be regarded by the rationalist as the workings of the imagination (i.e. illusory); astrologers or tarot readers may be regarded as having fertile imaginations (i.e. suffering from illusions), but to the mystic, or astrologer, their experiences are real. However, by using the word 'imagination' to describe the fount of these experiences, it is possible to entice the rationalist, who can accept the value of the imagination for what it is, a tool which, we shall see, is a key to unlocking the hidden dimensions of the unconscious. The right approach to the 'sixth sense' of the imagination is not to accept literally what its messages might tell us but to understand their symbolic nature. The unconscious speaks to us through the language of symbols, through our dreams and through the imagination, which may be used to form a meaningful link between the conscious and the unconscious self.

In establishing this 'creative' attitude to the imagination, it will become apparent that we are dealing with the nature of symbols and have a need to learn the language that they use in speaking to us, in communicating the depth of their meaning. A symbol is an image which not only evokes an intellectual response but also evokes feelings and stimulates the imagination. The 'meaning' of a symbol cannot be defined in the same way as a sign, which conveys a specific meaning or instruction. Symbols are evocative of a deep, personal response and often achieve this on account of their universal nature. The symbols of astrology have special psychological meaning and have virtually remained unchanged over thousands of years, although they have been refined and adapted to suit the needs of particular cultures and periods in the history of human development. What has really changed is the attitude towards their significance (symbols and the imagination are dealt with in greater depth in Chapter 2).

During the first half of this century, work initiated by Marc Edmund Jones and Dane Rudhyar precipitated a change in many astrologers' attitudes towards the stars and planets. They began to say that the planets no longer ruled us, but could be seen to act as guides for the journey of inner exploration. Relevant to this is the work of C.G. Jung who pointed out that the symbols of the zodiac were representations of inner, unconscious processes and archetypes that have been projected into the environment.

The ancient students of astrology saw the planets and the zodiac as gods. Following Jung, we now call these astrological gods 'archetypes'; these constitute the blueprint on which life is founded and they live in each and every one of us. Astrology is a sophisticated tool which can be used to mirror the processes of the unconscious and which can also be used as a guide through the unexplored realms of expanding consciousness.

Early in this century, psychologists claimed to have discovered that there is an aspect of the human mind that lies beyond the realm of consciousness, that is, the unconscious. From then on others have been naming curious aspects of the mind that are manifestations or 'messages' from the unconscious region. The unconscious, it has been discovered, 'talks' to us through symbols – through dreams and the imagination to the individual, through mythology and religious images to the race or culture. In particular, this book is concerned with the images presented to us by the ancient system of astrology.

The unconscious under many different guises has been a

recognised reality since time immemorial, but its significance is only just beginning to be recognised again, to be renamed by science.

Many people tend today to regard technology as basically an evil thing, the potential bringer of downfall, destruction, and world-wide disasters, from the uncontrollable release of nuclear radiation to lethal pollution of the earth affecting all living organisms. But it is immature to blame or fear technology, something which we ourselves have created, for the cause of the problem has a deeper root than this, one that is embedded in the human psyche.

We have not grown inwardly at the same rate as has our technical knowledge and ingenuity. The technologies of our world have taken a gigantic leap forward, while the development of understanding of the unconscious forces that control their power has hardly moved forward at all.

Despite the dangers that result from the misuse of sophisticated technology, it is a fact that in the Western world technology is giving many people the freedom to embark on the inner journey. This journey has limitless possibilities and the stage has now been reached where the first steps on it must be taken collectively to allow growth as a world family from adolescence to maturity. However, this process is one which must be discovered and undertaken first on an individual basis. Self-exploration and self-knowledge by the individual are steps along a path that should eventually lead to collective growth and maturity.

Self-knowledge is a difficult idea to define but one can say that what one should hope to achieve on seeking it is an expansion of consciousness and an awareness of new, unexplored dimensions of reality that exist within and which are accessible through hard work and commitment. This commitment to self-exploration is not only of value to the person who undertakes it. It is not a selfish process, for it should be seen as the means by which our race will evolve as a whole. It is therefore a task that demands a great sense of responsibility, for, by learning to move towards our own maturity

20

and wholeness, we are learning about the means by which humanity as a whole takes the same steps.

Most people's conception of time is of a flow in a uniform direction, such as moving from birth, through life, to death. Time is considered as moving in a straight line and with no connection to the events or objects of the material world that surround us. The implication of this, and in fact the way everyday reality is actually experienced, is that events and circumstances happen *to* us. We are surrounded by apparently disconnected phenomena taking place in the world 'out there', giving us a strong impression that the observer and the observed are separate, with no relationship, and both seem to have no influence on the passage of time, which continues on its way regardless.

This lack of connection or relationship between the observer and the events that the observer perceives is how everyday reality is experienced, and if this were not so then it would be extremely difficult to make any sense at all of the world in which we live. A world view predominates that demands objectivity and this results in the division of reality into opposites: the observer and the observed; mind and body; inner and outer; the conscious and unconscious.

The normal experience of everyday reality is bound up in this classical view of the world, which in recent times has been emphasised by the demands of science. Each fact about our world and ourselves that has been discovered by scientific method has been confirmed with strict objectivity. That is to say, scientific observations and experiments are only valid if the observer – the experimenter – has no influence on the outcome of the experiment. In this way the world can be observed as if we are not a part of it. This belief in the possibility of strict objectivity was strengthened by Sir Isaac Newton when he described the laws of nature in the seventeenth century. The laws of classical mechanics effectively separated all causes from the effects that they created, and led to the theory of a totally predictable world. If the laws of mechanics were true, it seemed to follow that all the

21

phenomena in the universe could in theory be predicted. The movement of the stars and planets as well as the processes of the human mind and body could be reduced to a set of equations and treated exactly as if they were a mechanical instrument. So successful was the mechanistic view of reality that the technology of today became possible, and with it the many benefits that proliferate in the developed Western cultures.

It is not an easy step to accept that this conception of the nature of reality is not able to give us a complete description of the apparently solid world perceived by our senses. But it is in fact only a limited description. A new world has been revealed by modern science, by the new physics that is delving into microcosmic subatomic particles and the macrocosmic realms of celestial mechanics. On an atomic level, the new physics describes reality in terms of the interconnectedness of all things, of objectivity as being an illusion and, more importantly for our current concern, of events and the objects of everyday reality not as 'things' but as processes which display patterns of probability.

Fred Alan Wolf comments[2] —

> Until the discoveries of modern quantum theory in this century, the physical universe and our thoughts about the physical universe were deemed to be totally separate. Quantum physics shows us that what we visualise is what we see. In other words, our thoughts about the world and the way the world appears are fundamentally related. The relationship between thought and 'reality' is, however, a subtle one. A chair is not just made up of little tiny ball-like atoms all jingling around. There are no atoms present until we actually begin to look for them. How is this possible? Well, first of all, atoms have no well-defined boundaries. These fuzzy little things only begin to appear with boundaries when we perform sophisticated experiments which actually destroy the chair.
>
> We have come to learn through quantum physics that *no* objects have well-defined boundaries. If we can imagine the

---

2. Bob Toben and Fred Alan Wolf, *Space-Time and Beyond*, Bantam. This is one of the most accessible works published on cosmic unity, scientific theory, and the nature of consciousness.

chair existing without us, just for a moment, its boundaries would become fuzzy too!

The world, according to this view, is not the mechanical one that might appear to our senses, but, in some mysterious way, the events that occur are connected to ourselves and we are a part of an unfolding process. No longer can we consider ourselves as innocent bystanders. By applying an understanding of the late twentieth century scientific view of reality to the fundamental laws of human behaviour and experience, the individual realises that he or she is not a separate entity from the surrounding world, and is not a mere observer, since by the very act of observation he or she affects the events that take place in the world as well as being affected by it.

Marilyn Ferguson in *The Aquarian Conspiracy* describes modern physics as revealing a reality that is very fluid, like the surrealistic melted clocks of Salvador Dali: 'Matter has only a "tendency to exist". There are no things, only connections. Only relationships.' Furthermore, Fritjof Capra explains[3] —

> Quantum theory . . . reveals a basic oneness of the universe. It shows that we cannot decompose the world into independently existing smallest units. As we penetrate into matter, nature does not show us any isolated 'basic building blocks', but rather appears as a complicated web of relations between the various parts of the whole. These relations always include the observer in an essential way. The human observer constitutes the final link in the chain of observational processes, and the properties of any atomic object can only be understood in terms of the object's interaction with the observer. This means that the classical ideal of an objective description of nature is no longer valid. The Cartesian partition between the I and the world, between the observer and the observed, cannot be made when dealing with atomic matter. In atomic physics, we can never

---

3. Fritjof Capra's *Tao of Physics* (Fontana) is perhaps the classic work on the relationships that exist between modern physics – quantum theory and relativity – and Eastern mysticism. Recent developments in subatomic physics have reinforced his thesis.

speak about nature without, at the same time, speaking about ourselves.

Atomic physicists describe the connections between sub-atomic particles in terms of probabilities and probability functions, which are the equations describing chance sub-atomic events; the equivalent psychological term applied to the happenings of everyday life is 'synchronicity', a term coined by Jung to describe the connections between apparently chance but meaningful occurrences. The word synchronicity, described by Jung as 'an acausal connecting principle'[4] is often confused with the word synchronous, which means occurring at the same time or at the same rate. Synchronicity between two events says nothing about the times at which they occur, but implies that there is a connection between them, *even when one does not appear to have caused the other* (hence the word 'acausal'). This does not mean that all apparently chance events are connected by synchronicity. The important factor is whether or not the events in question are meaningful to the person involved: a stranger passes me in the street, a chance event; a person I have not seen for ten years passes me in the street – a meaningful, chance event. Synchronicity implies that there is a holistic relationship between a physical event and a subjective one. The two events may coincide in time but they do not have to. Synchronicity on an everyday level is easy to observe by simply reinterpreting significant events which happen as if by chance. The telephone rings and a friend to whom you haven't spoken for years says he will be in town, and you respond by saying, 'It's strange – I was only thinking of you yesterday.' A chance occurrence, but

---

4. In *Synchronicity* by Prof. C.G. Jung (Routledge & Kegan Paul), Jung examines this psychic factor and draws far-reaching conclusions as to the nature of this principle. He also studies carefully the effectiveness of astrology. It was this short book that forced a reconsideration of the meaning of chance, probability and coincidence, and of the singular events in the life of an individual.

what patterns of unknown events led up to it? The connections are there, even if not directly observed.

The discoveries of the new physics have their counterparts in the schools of thought of Eastern mysticism – in Buddhism, particularly Zen Buddhism, in Hinduism and in the Chinese philosophy of Tao, or the 'Way'. The latter describes the reality of the world as a process of continuous change and that for human beings to live happily and to their fullest potential it is necessary to accept this flow of change and work with it. The 'opposites' also exist in this philosophy, but instead of being in conflict with one another and having no relationship they are to be understood as being polar opposites, two sides of the same coin. Not only this, but the process of continuous change is such that all things change eventually into their opposite in a cyclic manner that takes its precedent from the passing of the seasons and the cycle of night and day.

Alan Watts described this attitude in Eastern philosophy thus[5] —

> At the very roots of Chinese thinking and feeling there lies the principle of polarity, which is not to be confused with the ideas of opposition or conflict. In the metaphors of other cultures, light is at war with darkness, life with death, good with evil, and the positive with the negative, and thus an idealism to cultivate the former and be rid of the latter flourishes throughout much of the world. To the traditional way of Chinese thinking, this is as incomprehensible as an electric current without both positive and negative poles, for polarity is the principle that + and −, north and south, are different aspects of one and the same system, and that the disappearance of either one of them would be the disappearance of the system.
>
> People who have been brought up in the aura of Christian and Hebrew aspirations find this frustrating, because it seems to deny any possibility of progress, an ideal which flows from their linear (as distinct from cyclic) view of time and history. Indeed,

---

5. Alan Watts, *Tao – The Watercourse Way* (Penguin Books). As well as polarity, the philosophy of the Tao encompasses the idea of the cyclic nature of time. The Chinese believed there were two ideas of time, namely timeless time or eternity, unchanging eternity, with superimposed on it cyclic time. We live normally, in our consciousness, in cyclic time.

the whole enterprise of Western technology is 'to make the world a better place' – to have pleasure without pain, wealth without poverty, and health without sickness.

As an example of this process, consider the opposites of happiness and sadness. It is not possible to remain perpetually in either of these states and most of us tend to stay somewhere on the line between the two extremes. Do not envy persons who outwardly always appear ebullient and free from care, always with a smile and a pleasantry, for within them are contained the seeds of the opposite, operating on an unconscious level, and the happier they appear, the greater the potentially damaging tension between the two extremes. The Chinese philosophers said that we should strive neither for one extreme nor the other, but maintain a dynamic balance between the two and move with the tides as they flow from one to the other. If the polar opposites of health and disease are considered in this light, for example, then a completely different attitude must be developed towards illness which can only be understood in relative terms. This means that our definition of disease depends on what we mean by health and vice versa. No virtue can be considered absolute.[6]

A basic pair of polar opposites, which will be considered again later, are the masculine and feminine, not simply in terms of man and woman but of their attributes, such as the feminine ones of nurturing, receptivity, the unconscious, etc., and the masculine ones of extroversion, rational thought, consciousness, etc. The polar opposites of masculine and feminine can be explored as part of every individ-

---

6. Readers interested in the relevance of all this to health and healing will find much in the work of Larry Dossey, MD. His contribution is in describing the relevance of these ideas to human biology and in particular to his own field of health care. In his book *Space, Time & Medicine* (Shambhala), he describes how medicine has been reluctant to incorporate the ideas of modern physics, continuing to view the body as a clockwork mechanism. Perhaps the most profound of Dr Dossey's discussions concerns our belief that time 'flows' – a belief refuted by the new physics – and that this belief profoundly affects our health.

ual, whether man or woman, and together form a whole.

The aim now is to discover the nature of the relationship between the opposites, particularly between the inner and outer realms of experience, and also to learn about the pattern of change. How does it develop? What happens and when does it happen? What is the sequence of the process and how does one achieve and maintain a balance between the apparently opposing forces of nature? Answers to these questions will be of help in running our lives, in dealing with problems that arise and in growing to psychological and spiritual maturity.

The ancient system of astrology holds a key to these questions, for its symbols are based on the unfolding of patterns and cycles. Each of the planets is associated with a particular human quality, and the signs of the zodiac indicate the different ways that these qualities or energies can be expressed by the individual. The ancient philosophers who laid the foundations of astrology as it is known today observed the unconscious processes of their own minds by projecting them onto the stars and planets, where they were able to observe them as if they had an objective and independent reality. The notion was then developed that the stars and planets had a direct influence on human behaviour. Instead of regarding these influences as originating from the minds that created them, they were experienced as an external influence. The stars and planets were given the attributes of gods and goddesses who ruled over the human domains of love, work, health, home, aspirations, success and failure. Astrologers observed the effects of the planetary gods and goddesses not as consistently the same and unremitting but as cyclic in nature, the influence of Venus, for example, waxing and waning, increasing and decreasing, moving through crisis points, according to a period and sequence of cyclic events related to her own journey around the sun.

Despite the rejection of astrology by modern rationalism, it has in a paradoxical way helped to strengthen the old belief of planetary influences by emphasising the idea that anything that appears to be external, as far as our senses are concerned, or which is separate from the conscious self, has an independent, self-supporting, self-perpetuating reality of its own. This view of external planetary influences, still prevalent among many astrologers today, is the main reason why so many people reject astrology out of hand as having no real contribution to make to our understanding of everyday life.

Astrology must, in order to make any sense in modern terms, be reinterpreted in a manner that is consistent with the ideas of wholeness and of relationships existing between the individual's inner space and the outer space of sensual reality. Instead of influencing our everyday lives, the stars and planets reflect back to us the processes and cycles of unconscious growth and development of each individual throughout life. In other words, astrological symbols mirror the cycles of birth, growth, decay and rebirth occurring in every sphere of life, and to look into them is to look into the unconscious and see that what appears to be happening *to* us is actually happening *because of* us. The unconscious is everything that appears to be separated from the conscious self; it is the body and it is the material world of existence. It speaks to us through the imagination, which creates the symbols of astrology, and on this level becomes a means of perception, thus forming a bridge between the disconnected worlds of inner and outer experience.

It is a mistake to regard the unconscious as being a 'thing' that can be located in space and time. Although we speak of the unconscious as being 'in' the individual, this is only a manner of speaking for practical purposes. The unconscious as I have defined it is everything that is not conscious, that is, everything that we do not identify with the conscious ego. So to describe astrological influences as being images that are projected outwards from within is greatly to oversimplify the matter. I am not setting my theories in opposition to traditional astrological beliefs, but am applying a

28

theory which supports their foundations, but which does not, on the other hand, subscribe to 'outer influence'. The unconscious may not be 'inside' us, but neither is it 'outside' either. However, for the sake of convenience, and to conform with psychological theory, I refer to inner space, but without the connotation of this being actually inside anything or anyone. Rather it can be regarded as the reality behind or beyond external appearances.

The application of these ideas to astrology is described by Peter Lemesurier[7] —

> I do not deny that you may have chosen to be born under a particular configuration of sun, moon and planets – the same configuration, perhaps, under which your soul last left the earth-planes. If so it would not be too surprising if that configuration in turn, like the shape of your head or the lines on your palm, reflected to some extent your foreknowledge of your own fate.
>
> I do not deny, either, that there may be unseen links between the movements of the heavens and the phenomena of the terrestrial sphere. The assumption . . . was certainly basic to the science of the ancient world, and it is reflected in our own day in the Jungian notion of synchronicity. In which case it would not be too surprising if your own fortunes were linked to the movements of the heavenly bodies, just as they apparently are to everything else.
>
> Nor do I deny the possibility that those skilled in such things may be able to use their knowledge of the heavens to enable you to bring to the surface of consciousness your own deeper knowledge of your destiny . . .
>
> All these things are as may be. But it is perhaps worth remembering that the heavenly vault and the wheeling galaxies are not there to serve you. Rather are you there to serve the universe. And in particular the signs of the zodiac, you may be sure, were not devised to enable you or me to dabble in personal fortune-telling.
>
> But note the word 'devised'. For the signs of the zodiac have no independent existence. The stars do not form patterns. Their distribution across the night sky is quite random. There are no Twins, no Bull, no Ram, no Fishes, no Water-Carrier. It is we

---

7.   Peter Lemesurier's *Gospel of the Stars* (Compton Press) is a book about the zodiac as an expression by humankind of our destiny through the succeeding ages of our planet.

who create those patterns; we who then impose them on the stars. The pictures that we see in the upside-down teacup of the heavens are images of our own devising. It is man's own thoughts that are out there among the stars.

As we join up the dots of the celestial star-puzzle, interpret the ink-blots of the ultimate in Rorshach tests, what are revealed to us are the secrets not of outer but of inner space. The limitless inner space of our own consciousness. The unfathomable well of human vision and foreknowledge.

By looking outwards we see inwards.

And so, by contemplating the dance of the galaxies, the rhythms of the universe, we may start to gain new insights into man's real nature. For he is inevitably part of that universe. Its rhythms are his rhythms. Its cycles are his cycles. It is the very pendulum of the cosmic clock that makes man tick.

Seeing the life of the unconscious through the symbols found in the stars and planets is called 'projection'. This is a process whereby the inner energies of the psyche are projected onto and into things that exist in the outside world. Projection does not only apply to the archetypal qualities given to the stars and planets but occurs on every level, including, of course, the ascribing to objects, people and events qualities which are not necessarily theirs but which we see in them.

Projection can be a valuable means of observing those areas of our own personalities that function on an unconscious level. Unfortunately, those particular parts that we fail to recognise in ourselves are usually those which we do not like, the negative character traits such as meanness, stupidity and so on.

So what is the key for recognising the process of projection? Over-reaction to an emotional stimulus is a sure sign of a projection. One person may recognise but accept the stupidity of someone; another may react violently against it. The latter is usually the unwitting hypocrite. Watch for the over-reaction in yourself. If you are incensed at your loved one's stupidity, then in some way you are being very stupid and this unconscious deed is being projected onto a perhaps accepting hook.

30

Superstition of every kind is born from the process of projecting unconscious energies as in the situation described on page 15. The irrational practices that result can have a considerable hold on susceptible individuals. There are others on the other hand who remain unaffected, and this is not surprising as many people nowadays are completely disconnected from their own unconscious urges and passions. They see nothing in astrology but mere superstition, and dismiss it as nonsense (and they are by no means entirely wrong!).

The salient question perhaps is not how or why does astrology work, but why should it influence the lives of so many believers, while others do not respond to it at all. The answer is rather a complicated one and partly tied up with projection. Experiencing the influence of astrology, the apparent influence of the stars and planets, gives one the opportunity to recognise connections that stem from within. These celestial outer forces may or may not have an immediate relationship with ourselves, but they have certainly become part of our own psychic make-up. In recognising this, and in learning to form a proper relationship with the forces of the cosmos, it becomes possible to work with them, to take control of life, instead of being endlessly blown about by the whims of fate and circumstance. Learning this proper relationship can be done in many ways; one such way is by understanding the archetypal energies and forces represented to us by the astrological symbols of the planets and the zodiac.

Without developing this sort of relationship between the inner and outer worlds of experience, the patterns of life simply repeat themselves and the individual is forced to repeat the same unsatisfactory circumstances over and over again, without seeing that circumstances are repeated because the individual is out of touch, is disconnected from their cause. Everyone is prone to this process to a lesser or greater degree and it is much easier to see it happening in other people than to observe it in oneself.

One particular area where the effects of repeating patterns is most apparent is in the field of relationships. The typical pattern begins with the choice of a partner who appears at first to embody the ideal person, but whose negative traits seem to become more and more exaggerated as time goes on so as to be the cause of a final separation. The pattern will go on repeating itself, until the individual concerned recognises that the *repeating* problem is his or her own. When dealt with, the relationship can then move on to the next phase of its evolution.

A male friend of mine who is now 39 years old is still progressing through relationships of the kind that he had when a teenager, without any of them developing to a further level of maturity. At the end of the cycle there comes a crisis point in which he has the choice of either dealing with and thus helping the relationship to mature or ending it and starting all over again. My friend always chooses the latter course – but there is no necessity.

In summary, the first step to inner growth is the recognition of a pattern in outer circumstances, whether it be to do with career, money, relationships, health and so on. These patterns are represented in astrology by the planets, each having its own orbital period, each representing a different archetypal force (see Chapter 5). How these forces operate and manifest themselves in the life of the individual is expressed by the signs of the zodiac (see Chapter 7) and the areas of life in which their effects are experienced are indicated by the astrological houses (see Chapter 6).

In the next chapter I will further explain the value of learning about the underlying cycles and patterns of life.

CHAPTER 2
PATTERNS OF INNER GROWTH

Personal circumstances are a reflection of the inner state of mind, and just as the physical body grows to maturity so does the inner self. Patterns of this inner growth are reflected in the circumstances that we create in everyday life, so, to make sense of what is happening, it is necessary to explore the inner worlds. The language of the inner worlds of experience utilises symbols, dreams and the imagination, and gives a basis for our understanding of astrology. With this understanding, working with dreams and explorative methods of visualisation, using the planetary symbols, are described.

Once upon a time I dreamt I was a butterfly fluttering hither and thither, to all intents and purposes, a butterfly. I was conscious only of following my fancies (as a butterfly) and I was unconscious of my individuality as a man. Suddenly I was awakened and there I lay, myself again. I do not know whether I was then dreaming I was a butterfly or whether I am now a butterfly dreaming that I am a man.

Chuang Tzu

The eternal quest for truth and the reality behind life presents us with the same problem that the Eastern mystic Chuang Tzu had to face. Is the life we know just as we perceive it to be through our waking senses, or is it just a dream from which one day we shall awaken and discover the true nature of ourselves? And then, once we have awoken, how will we know that it is not yet another dream?

This awakening process is an allegory that describes the search for ourselves.

It has always struck me as being rather strange that dreams or the imagination are so difficult for us to understand. Other messages from the body or nervous system seem so obvious – an easily identifiable message originating in the stomach indicates hunger, a painful ache in the head indicates the need to rest or relieve tension – but what on earth do dreams mean? And now there is even the added confusion that we don't even know if we ourselves are living in a dream!

During the first half of this century, Sigmund Freud and Carl Jung, among others, had laid the foundation for an approach to understanding and making use of dream symbolism in helping the individual to learn more about the nature of his or her self. It was shown that the presence of autonomous processes going on in the unconscious could be detected by their emergence through the symbols of dreams or the imagination. Freud's approach was limited, although his contributions to our present knowledge are beyond value in establishing that within the human psyche there is an area with content and activity of which we are not conscious, the area which Freud called the subconscious.

Jung's approach was eclectic and not dogmatic, and more in tune with and also a direct stimulus for the development of modern depth, humanistic and transpersonal psychologies. The major significance of dream interpretation is only just beginning to be appreciated. It is being found to relate specifically to many activities and fields developing rapidly once more: astrology, the I Ching, tarot, palmistry, psychic readings, inner journeys and 'far memory', to name but a few. Light is also now being shed on the significance of traditional studies of the mind that were in danger of becoming outdated and were suffering from loss of relevance – the symbols had lost their energy.

Not only can dreams be of value in self-discovery, but also the methods and approach to dream analysis can be applied to an understanding of life itself, to the dream in which we all live and from which we are awakening into a new reality, a New Age, helped by an understanding of our own personal symbols.

Symbols should express a meaning that is much greater than the symbol outwardly shows. If this is not the case, if it does not represent a form of consciousness, it is merely what we would call a sign, which is a convenient, concise way of conveying a specific instruction. The meaning of a symbol is never exact or specific because it needs interpreting and the interpretation will depend on the interpreter's personal reaction to it.

Every symbol has what is called an archetypal meaning and a personal meaning. To clarify this, let's return to the butterfly.

The archetypal meaning of this particular symbol is connected with freedom of the spirit, of metamorphosis from the earthly caterpillar into a winged creature of such delicate beauty that it is impossible to describe – perhaps like the idea we have of the true spirit or true essence of ourselves.

Psyche in Greek mythology, the beloved of Eros, was represented as having butterfly wings. The archetypal aspect of the butterfly symbol may be described, then, as spirit or freedom, a meaning of the symbol which we might agree upon. But in addition, no two people would visualise or picture exactly the same representation of a butterfly when asked to do so. Each person draws on the sum total of his or her own experience, his or her present 'condition', when visualising or painting a butterfly – or understanding the symbolic meaning of the butterfly. The qualities given to the butterfly reveal the condition of the person who gave it content. One person's butterfly will be small, grey and moth-like, another's will be colourful and fly freely through the air. This is the personal aspect of a symbol and can be used as a mirror for the personality.

Here is another example. We recognise the rose as an archetypal symbol of love, but love means many things to many people, and likewise no two people would paint or visualise exactly the same rose. The archetypal meaning of a symbol is its essence. The personal meaning of a symbol is the content which each person gives to it, the way it is *seen*, and this is an individual experience enabling the personal form or expression of a symbol to be used as a mirror of the self.

It is not just our dreams that contain significant symbols, but the processes of the imagination too.

The meaning of the word 'imagination' causes confusion because we have come to regard the imaginary as something that has no reality.

And so we frequently come across persons who dismiss the products of the imagination as nothing more than fantasy, or wishful thinking, especially if they happen to have a well developed intellect. The intellect may try to analyse and rationalise the products of the imagination, which will seem inevitably irrational because the intellect has such a high regard for logic, order and rationality. It simply cannot encompass the significance of these 'irrational' and therefore distasteful products of the imagination which it denigrates and, in so doing, destroys their potential for illuminating the workings of the unconscious, which are themselves non-rational by nature. The result is a 'type' of person who views the imagination as nothing more than a compensation for the comparatively drab world of rationality and objective thought which, at its extreme, is a clockwork world that may be reduced ultimately to nothing more than equations and the deterministic laws of mechanics.

Because the imagination is often undervalued and underdeveloped, this aspect of the psyche may also be repressed and even operate autonomously without the individual being aware of it. In this instance, the repressed contents of the psyche make their presence known by projection into the outside world, where they cling to a person or thing as if they were part of its objective reality. These projected contents of the imagination may not be recognised as a part of the consciousness that projects them, but are incorrectly perceived as an external reality.

The individual may then have great difficulty in distinguishing what is an objective reality from what is purely subjective, stemming from personal feelings. Thus a conditioned response may falsely be assumed to be based on an objective truth which is alluded to as a 'fact' when it is not. A lack of discrimination is also manifest when a person accepts that something is true simply because somebody says that it is true, firing the imagination and stimulating its projection into the world of objective experience. When objective and subjective are confused we find the many rampant 'beliefs' about the nature of reality that can never be proven one way or another, for they are clouded by a projected product of the mind. I might believe that cats are beautiful, friendly creatures. You might believe that they are horrible and vicious. Are cats friendly or vicious?

My intention is not to belittle the projection of personal prejudices but simply to discover the process at work, to obtain a better understanding of the nature of their reality.

The imagination can be used actively in meditation in a manner that is directly analogous to the dream experience, but where the 'dreamer' is awake. Therefore a knowledge of the nature of dreams would help us to understand the visualisation techniques called creative or 'active' imagination. In addition, a knowledge of dream interpretation is a great help in understanding the subjective process at work in the personal unconscious and also in interpreting external symbols that refer to an individual – such as the astrological symbols of the birth chart. Often it is found that the symbolism of dreams bears a direct relationship to astrological and alchemical symbolism.

We have undertaken the task of uniting the apparently separated worlds of inner and outer experience. This is the result of developing an expanded consciousness which encompasses mind and body, inner and outer. So what is the nature of the relationship existing between these two worlds? Perhaps the properties of our dreams can show this and they are therefore well worth examining in this context.

Events which occur in the outer world that have a connection with our personal lives may be treated as the dreams in which we live. Now regardless of whether we are considering the dreams that live in us, or the dreams in which we live, the approach to understanding 'the dream' is the same.

The nature of dreams is similar to that of the imagination, which may be regarded as a 'waking' dream. They differ in that during the waking state the ego is able to exercise a shaping process, which gives a rational imprint of sequence in time and modifies the 'waking' dream of the imagination into a cohesive picture. The 'sleeping' dream is closer to the timeless dimensions of the unconscious and is a purer representation of it, for the dream has not yet been moulded to fit in with our normal perception of reality, as described or defined by the conscious ego.

For the rest of this chapter, the word 'dream' and 'symbol' may be taken as synonymous, remembering also that astrology is based on a system of interrelated symbols. This will be of help later when the astrological cycles and patterns are examined in detail.

To the rational mind then, dreams make no sense. A different approach is needed. A dream should be experienced as if it were a poem or a fairytale. It must be accepted and its effect allowed to work its charms upon us. Its themes and content may be discussed and amplified, personal associations may be made to it and above all, its *purpose* discerned.

The meaning of a dream needs to be drawn out, dwelt upon and brought fully into the light of day so that it does not slip mistily back into the darker recesses of the mind. We must be wary of the critical aspect of the analytical mind at work, which tends to ignore, dismiss, destroy and close down the doors of perception rather than lead to a wider understanding of the nature of consciousness and the opening of these doors.

The modern paradigm for understanding our world and its phenomena demands a definable link between a cause and its predictable effect. This approach applied to the understanding of dreams is helpful, but limited. It is an approach which looks for the common cause of all the manifestations of a dream. I take a bus ride and that night I dream that I am on a journey. The cause of the dream, or the initial impulse, was probably my waking experience of the journey by bus. I have discovered the cause of the effect. But in the same way that it is not enough to discover about a poem what the initial impulse for its creation might have been, the causal significance of a dream gives only a part of the story. In order to reveal the significance of this dream, it is necessary to ask what is its *aim or purpose*, what lies behind the unconscious activity which stimulated this dream.

The details are important. The dream was not just about a bus, it was a red bus. Why red? It was going fast, and was crowded, stuffy and likely to veer off the road any minute. Why these conditions? What aspect of myself is crowded, stuffy and likely to have an accident if it continues at its present speed? And when this question can be answered, the purpose of the dream may become apparent.

Applying this mode of understanding to the interpretation of astrological symbols, it becomes clear that it is not enough to look for a planetary influence, for example, but to seek the purpose and aim of a meaningful 'chance' configuration.

The planetary pattern occurring at the time of a person's birth as represented by the birth chart might seem like a chance configuration, but it is more than mere chance, it is *meaningful chance*, what we have been calling synchronicity (see pages 24–5) for it has a specific relationship to the individual concerned. It is his or her own unique pattern. It is now necessary to ask what is the purpose that can be discovered by making this meaningful link. When asking a question such as this, we are assuming that a symbol has a definite, purposeful relationship with the future, that has its roots in the past. This means that a symbol will be created from past events and circumstances, but its interpretation, its meaning, is directed towards informing the individual about his or her *future*. For example, someone might dream of a catastrophe of some sort. This may be interpreted that the dreamer's past actions are leading to a future catastrophe. The dream gives the dreamer an opportunity to modify his or her circumstances so that this future event might be avoided, or at least prepared for.

The causal approach to understanding dreams is concerned with the past (the cause happens before the effect) and hence the preliminary preoccupation in dream analysis with the history of the individual concerned. This preoccupation stretches back not only to the occurrences of the previous few days or weeks but often way back into childhood where root causes may be sought for the unconscious condition, as represented by a dream.

Where the influence of the dreamer's past is being considered in relation to the dream, it is found that the dream's content can indicate the expression of desires or experiences that have been suppressed from consciousness, which have then taken on an autonomous role in the unconscious and which now make their presence known through the medium of the dream. The classic example of this causal approach is the interpretation of a dream in which many of its contents appear to be allusions to sexual organs, the male organ being represented by tall buildings, pencils, guns, etc., or the female organ by any form of receptacle. They may all seem to have a sexual cause and implication, perhaps expressions of wish fulfilment that could have been denied since childhood, and be a multiple manifestation of a single cause.

This is fine, but does not take the story far enough, for the conscious ego is constantly moving through the time domain in the direction of the future and the dream may be viewed as guidance for this future direction. We must ask why a particular symbol was chosen. Why a tall building

40

rather than a gun? Why a crowded bus rather than an empty one? When this difference becomes meaningful for the dreamer, it becomes clear that the nature of the dream content (and therefore of the unconscious itself of which the dream acts as ambassador) is *compensatory*, which I shall now explain.

Where the conscious mind is positive, the unconscious is relative to it and negative, and vice versa. This relative and compensatory role of the unconscious always indicates a movement or drive towards a form of wholeness and balance. The symbols expressed in dreams reveal the compensation necessary to the conscious self, in order that it can function in its optimum state of health or effectiveness.

Two forms of compensation occur. The first is where the opposite condition of the personality is represented. For example, a person leading a highly active, full life that allows little time for rest and self-contemplation may dream of being in peaceful country surroundings where there is nothing to distract the dreamer from appreciating the beauty of his inner surroundings, of his own self. A person leading a dull, routine life may see himself in a dream as a hero figure, perhaps the driver of a fast car, winning glory and acclaim. In these two examples, the compensatory function is providing an awareness of the polar opposite to the waking condition, thus drawing attention to a psychological imbalance.

The second form of compensatory activity is such that the waking condition is exaggerated, a sort of negative compensation. For example, a person whose approach to life is too egocentric, may be represented in a dream that reveals him as emperor of a vast kingdom, where loyal subjects grovel to be of service and his every wish is their command. The compensatory function here is ridiculing the conscious situation, with the purpose that it be reduced rather than built up. Even though the overt nature of the dream is exaggeration, its purpose is that of compensating an ego-view that is far too one-sided.

It is easy to oversimplify the compensatory relationship of the unconscious to the ego, which are not necessarily simply opposites. For example, as the natural drive within the psyche is towards wholeness, the relative contents of these two polar opposites may be *complementary* rather than opposite. The opposite of a man is a woman, but the complementary function, relative to a man, may be represented as the son. In the circle of the zodiac, opposite zodiacal signs form 'wholes' together and are complementary. If examined, one discovers that opposite signs are of the same, not opposite, polarity. For example, Leo and Aquarius complement one another. They are also both masculine energies.

As contents of the unconscious, expressed through the symbols that occur in dreams, are compensatory, they do of course relate to the situation of the conscious personality. Therefore in order to explore a dream it is necessary to have a full understanding of the personal situation of the individual concerned. We need to know as much as possible about his or her outer life and outwardly expressed personality.

This last statement applies equally well to understanding any symbol as well as those in the dream experience. For example, an interpretation of astrological symbols and their relationship with the particular person to whom they refer will be completely meaningless if the situation of the individual cannot be related to the symbol, in order to clothe it with meaning.

Symbols represent an underlying pattern or energy. They are the images through which we can become aware of the archetypes, the gods that inhabit the unconscious, which is a store of primitive and instinctive behaviour patterns. Although a symbol may be a single image, such as a rose, or a butterfly, it can also be a personification, as, for example, the mythological figures of Venus, Mars, or Jupiter. Living symbols, such as these, have patterns of behaviour; they are known to be loving, warlike, benevolent, etc. Because their attributes are predictable, it is possible to say that they conform to a pattern of behaviour, and this is why we can say that symbols in general represent an underlying pattern. In dreams they are spontaneous representatives of the unconscious. This underlying reality must be given content by the individual in order to establish a relationship between the underlying pattern (the content of the unconscious) and the external circumstances.

In the case of an interpretation of the astrological symbols in a birth chart, for example, an individual will see himself mirrored by them but may believe that his personality has been influenced by an external cosmic source, rather than recognising that it is he who has created the link. This creating of a link is the very process that we are chasing; it is the formation of a bridge between the dissociated worlds of the conscious mind and the unconscious and it is a bridge that needs to be built or created, rather than being one that can be discovered to exist already. Science mocks the influence of the stars and planets, for the scientist cannot discover the link. It does not exist until it is *created* by a conscious and concerted effort of the will and the imagination.

Remember that the stars do not conform to a pattern – the images of the zodiac were created by human beings. The images themselves are, however, far from being random; they have been developed into a cohesive, complex system over a period of thousands of years. Hence, the birth chart will reveal those archetypes that are common to all of us, and will be given particular meaning by the individual who interprets them. This process of interpreting symbols is exactly the same, whether it be of a birth chart, a tarot spread, or a dream.

Ultimately, the dreamer must come to terms with his or her own dreams and the main emphasis on interpretation of a personal symbol must be on this linking process. This we know is difficult, for symbols often express aspects of the self which the individual does not wish to see. They may be distasteful and therefore the dreamer may censor associations with the dream images which represent repressed contents of the unconscious.

We have seen how dreams should be regarded as having a purpose or intent, so that in the future the dreamer may avoid any unbalanced tendency or outlook. This directs our attention to the prophetic aspect of dreams, which not only reflect the current situation of the self, based on past occurrences, but also indicate the future outcome of events. In other words, dreams seem to know much better than we do what the future holds in store.

A dream may indicate disaster to a person who is working beyond his or her capacity to do so without suffering eventual ill effects. That person may well be the last to recognise this situation even though it had been foreseen and was being indicated by the unconscious for a long time. If the message cannot penetrate and goes unheeded, the person may realise what is happening only when it is too late. I do not mean to say that the purpose of a prophetic symbol is to predict the *definite* occurrence of a future event. Its purpose is to reflect the present situation so that if the current path is continued the outcome is clarified. Disaster may be averted if the necessary steps are taken, otherwise it may be an inevitable outcome as in the example quoted.

The content of dreams often follows definite motifs that appear time and time again and which can be traced to a common foundation or source. It is here once more that we meet the formative principles of the unconscious known as the archetypes which have their correspondence with the motifs of astrology, mythology, religion, etc.

When the personal layer has been worked through, it is possible to delve down to a 'deeper' layer of the unconscious represented by the dream's motifs and this layer is the collective unconscious. The word 'collective' indicates that there is an aspect of the unconscious psyche whose content is common to all and this content for the sake of convenience can be classified in such a manner that certain themes or motifs may be identified, and it is upon these that the personal content of the dream symbols is built. They are the blueprint on which the foundations of the personality are built.

The themes and motifs that thread their way through mythologies, religious systems and folklore often make their presence known in dream experiences, even though the individual may be unaware of their significance or origin. But it is usually this type of dream experience that has most effect on the individual for its underlying purpose is backed by the power of something that has much greater significance than the individual's experience of life.

The archetype which is often encountered in dreams is the spirit or soul figure, the anima or animus. The anima is the unconscious female elements within a man, whereas the animus is the male counterpart within a woman. The anima when personified is the male's view of · woman – what makes her female – and the animus is the female's equivalent view of 'maleness'. The anima and animus will be described again in more detail (see page 73). This particular archetype appears to guard the 'borderline' between the conscious and the unconscious self and is often personified as an unknown male (animus) or female (anima) figure, often in their negative or 'shadow' aspect.

This is so even if the personification in a dream is of someone whom the dreamer knows in waking life, for this indicates that a quality of the unconscious is being seen in that person and assumed to be part of him or her, rather than as a part of the dreamer's own personality. It is a particular approach to the understanding of dreams that their content should be understood as belonging completely to the dreamer, for, to Jung, who stressed the importance of interpretation on the subjective level, 'the dream is a spontaneous self-portrayal in symbolic form of the actual situation in the unconscious.'

When dealing with one's own dreams, it is important to keep a descriptive record, and not just for the reason that the memory of them tends to fade as they slip back into the dark areas of the unconscious. Often there is an unfolding pattern to observe which can reveal a deeper, elusive significance that becomes apparent only later when the pattern reveals itself. The language of a dream may seem to be indicating something other than its true purpose or aim, but a series of dreams may show the content to be circling around a particular centre which is never stated overtly, but only implied or hinted at.

The circular nature of dreams and their tendency to steer around a subject that is not expressed directly is analogous to the process of life itself, to the dream of life. Often we arrive at a particular conclusion or set of circumstances by an incredibly complex sequence of events. It is only in retrospect that the apparently incongruous events can be seen to fit into a pattern that was leading all the time to a particular condition or point of awareness. How often has one thought that in retrospect it would have been so much easier to go straight to the point and purpose of a situation, without having those of learning experiences that circumvent, but which eventually fall into a meaningful pattern, indicating the central purpose of life's circumstances. It is only when there is a pattern that a point of enlightenment can be arrived at.

Armed now with some basic information about dreams and their interpretation, we can turn to a practical method of inner exploration and consciousness expansion based on our ability to create inner imaginative symbols, pictures and thoughts.

The initiation into the mysteries of inner exploration is a simple one. The technique that I shall describe is now well known and used in many schools of psychology. It employs the inner process of imagination to visualise symbols, which can be observed with the inner eye and interpreted as if they were the product of a dream. This technique is described under various names, including active imagination, guided imagery, creative visualisation, guided fantasy, or path working. The latter term is used by schools of magick, whose rituals include a major element of this use of the imagination, which has now been adopted by schools of psychology. The experience is very similar to day-dreaming, the significant difference being that the subject does not drift into the experience but has a definite purpose in mind, perhaps a particular facet of the unconscious mind that the individual wishes to explore.

First, here is a preparatory exercise, a lesson in relaxation. Assume a comfortable position, preferably lying down in a warm, peaceful environment and relax. A useful technique for relaxation is to begin at the toes and slowly work up through the legs, abdomen, body, shoulders, arms, neck, head, etc., consciously attempting to relax each in turn. If any resistance or muscle tension is located, then this should be relaxed by first *tightening* the muscle even more and then relaxing it, imagining that the tension flows away after a blockage has been released. Pay particular attention to the neck, shoulders and head area, for these tend to get particularly tensed up during the course of normal activity. Make sure the teeth are not clenched together and that you are breathing evenly.

The next stage is to direct attention to the gradual rising and falling of the breath and to contemplate its rhythmic involuntary action.

This contemplation throws into relief the existence of an inner, peaceful, still centre, an aspect of the self which has no movement and is a point of pure self-consciousness. The subject should contemplate this still centre until completely relaxed. I use the word contemplate here rather than meditate because the process I am about to describe is not one of strict discipline and an emptying of the mind so that consciousness may be focused on a single point, as in the disciplines of meditative yoga; instead it is one whereby the walls of the conscious ego are softened somewhat so that the dream images of the imagination may enter. In this relaxation it is not necessary to still or repress thoughts, a feat that needs much practice and discipline, but simply to watch them, to act as an observer and study what they are, to let them drift into consciousness, follow them for a while and then allow them to drift away.

Now in this relaxed condition, visualise a rose with the inner eye. Create and paint a picture of a rose and contemplate its beauty for a while, allowing its form to change or grow as it wishes to do so. Paint as much detail in your mind about the rose as you can and imagine that you are really there watching it; you are able to smell its scent and reach out and touch it. Take careful note of its colour, size, the surroundings and anything else that appears in your imagination.

Now imagine that you look into the centre of the rose and find a jewel at its heart. Contemplate the meaning of the jewel that you have found at the centre of this flower. Now imagine that the jewel begins to radiate many hues of coloured light and that this light fills you and surrounds you as a coat of white light, sealing you within its aura. And, if you like, imagine finally that you radiate this light out into the universe, a light that represents love and peace. This is the end of the preparatory exercise.

This exercise is useful as an introduction for three reasons. First, it gives a useful relaxation technique that can be used at any time for whatever inner work is to be undertaken. Secondly, it is a useful psychic healing meditation that seals the aura against any unwanted difficult energy releases and prevents draining of energy. Indeed, it can be quite a useful exercise to perform if you want to revitalise yourself.

Thirdly, the exercise demonstrates the simple process of using the imagination to create a symbol, arising from the unconscious. The rose is an archetypal symbol representing the self, and also love in its earthly form. The manner in which the individual's rose is 'painted' depends purely on the individuality of that person. In order to obtain a better understanding of such a symbol it could be painted rather than simply visualised in contemplation. But the advantage

48

of the contemplative method is that the symbol can be allowed to grow, move, change and evolve, hence the name 'active imagination'.

Taking the process one stage further, it becomes apparent that if the inner symbols are personified – visualised in the form of people – then a line of communication and feedback can be established between the conscious self and the unconscious.

This is a difficult step for some as it may seem somewhat eccentric to talk or communicate with a figment of the imagination and it is not until the process is experienced that its validity becomes apparent. The unconscious often presents archetypal forms as personified in dreams. All that is being suggested here is that this be done through the use of the creative imagination. The next example exercise will make this clear.

After the preliminary relaxation exercise, imagine that you are in a cave. Spend a few minutes building up a picture of a cave in your mind, with you in it. Try to find out as much about the cave as you can experience. How big is it? Is it comfortable being in the cave, is it dark or light, of what texture and colour are the walls and the floor underfoot? Try to be in the cave as much as possible, touching, hearing, smelling and seeing. Don't watch yourself being in the cave, but imagine that you are really there.

Next you find a doorway to the left of the cave that you did not notice was there before and you pass through, out into the countryside, or whatever scene lies beyond. It is daytime. Spend time building up an experience in your imagination of yourself in the countryside. What is the weather like? Are there fields and hedgerows? What's the ground like? Is it hilly or flat? How far can you see?

Imagine that a friendly animal or bird comes to you and wishes to take you off somewhere. Take whatever creature occurs to you first and take note of what sort of creature it is that acts as your guide. Follow the creature and imagine you talk to it, asking it not to lead you astray, but to take you straight to its goal. Eventually you realise that the creature is leading you towards a figure standing in the distance. The figure is too far away for you to be able to discern any detail yet, but as you draw closer you realise that this person, to whom the creature is leading you, is very wise, knows much about you and will be able to help you as a guide through the unknown.

Approach your Guide and greet him or her. Spend the next few minutes trying to build up as much detail in your mind as you can about your Guide. Don't worry if you can't picture any vivid details, especially about the face, for these will come with time, practice and familiarity. What is the Guide wearing? How old is he or she? How is the Guide reacting towards you, with friendship or animosity? This last question is important. It does not matter what feelings you may have about this figure that you have created, but it does matter what he or she feels about you. Some people resent the idea of a wise aspect of themselves or the possibility that somebody may know them better than they do. The Guide should want to help and be concerned about your welfare. If you get the impression that this is not so, then you have possibly imagined a false guide and, if this is so, you should then look over the shoulder of this figure and imagine that you see another in the distance, to whom you should go, and repeat the procedure.

When you are satisfied that you have found the Guide figure that symbolises your own inner wisdom, you can begin to communicate with the Guide and receive answers. You may have difficulty understanding how this is possible. It is simply a process of imagining that you ask a question and that you receive a reply. You do all the work, although it is always important to accept whatever image or words come to you first during these exercises. You should not apply any censorship or discrimination, but accept totally the first impulses of your creative imagination. What is the Guide called? Where does he or she come from and what are the Guide's hopes or aims? Don't reject anything that is obvious or apparently ridiculous – it is important to be receptive and open to the often irrational promptings of the unconscious. If you have any difficulty obtaining a desired result or a reply at any time, give the Guide permission to go ahead. This may sound trite but it's a trick that usually works.

When you are ready, ask the Guide to bring the Sun to you in the form of a person and imagine next that the Sun materialises in front of you in the form of a living being. Again, create and examine the Sun in as much detail as possible. What is the Sun wearing, how do you feel about the Sun and how does he or she feel about you? If the Sun does not materialise in the form that you expect, again you should not censor it, but accept fully whatever comes to you.

Another point worth mentioning at this stage is that when dealing with archetypal personifications the aim is not to visualise people who are known in real life. This would show that a quality associated with that particular archetype is being projected onto the known person and attributed to that person, rather than being recognised as an aspect of the archetypal nature of the unconscious.

Ask the Sun what he or she needs from you and also ask the Sun to give you a symbol that represents a gift from the Sun to you. Take whatever occurs to you first and ask the Sun to explain the meaning of the symbol and how it can be used in your real life to benefit you. You can also bring the Guide in again here to explain further the meaning and use of the Sun's gift.

There is much healing energy in the archetype of the Sun, symbol of the deep centre, the higher Self, and this can be released as follows.

Form a circle of hands with the Guide on your left and the Sun to your right and imagine that the Guide and the Sun also join hands to complete the circle. Ask the Sun to give you as much of his or her life energy as you are able to take and imagine that the Sun begins to vibrate with light that grows in brightness and intensity, traverses around the circle and enters into you. Imagine that you become filled with this light. When you are ready, imagine that the radiation begins to die down and that you finally thank the Sun and the Guide for being with you.

Take careful note of your surroundings so that you can build them up in your imagination again at any time and, when you are ready, return to the cave from where you started and then slowly return your consciousness to the room in which you are lying or sitting, and open your eyes.

Before going any further, it is important to make a written record of this preliminary 'inner journey', for the experience, like a dream, easily slips back into the unconscious recesses of the mind and writing it all down helps to ground it for future reference. Also, one can begin associating immediately with the images and experiences that occurred and it is important to make a record of any difficulties that were encountered, as well as the descriptive material of what was visualised. Often, what didn't happen is just as significant as what did happen in revealing the possibility of blocked energy or a refusal by the ego (you!) to face up to an aspect of itself that is struggling to remain unconscious.

If these exercises are conducted over a period of time, it will be discovered how the changes that occur are significant in reflecting the processes that are at work in the unconscious. Hence, a written record acts as a diary giving an account of the sequence of experiences as well as the detail of their content. If you want to experience this exercise, don't read any more until you have done so, in order that my following comments do not affect the result.

This imagery technique can be developed by regarding each of the planetary archetypes, represented by astrological symbolism, as a particular aspect of the psyche which can be personified, focused on and worked with as an independent entity. But before going further into this (particularly later, in Chapter 7), I need to say more about the preliminary exercise in order to give you a greater insight into what lies behind it.

The cave represents in this case a means of moving from the rational world of consciousness into the more nebulous realm of the imagination through which contact with the unconscious can be established. The entry into a cave in dreams or creative imagination often symbolises the way through from the world of light and consciousness into the dark, unknown depths of the unconscious that lie beyond. In this case, the darkness is illumined by entry into the open scenery that lies beyond the cave as the 'explorer' passes through the door on the left (a leftward movement is towards the unknown, the unconscious, whereas the opposite indicates movement towards the known and the light of consciousness).

When visualising the scene that lies beyond the cave, the explorer often encounters water flowing nearby, perhaps a river or even the sea, classic symbols of contact with unconscious energies. It is important that the explorer is *in* the scene as much as possible, which is why I stressed the importance of seeing, touching, smelling and feeling as much as possible.

The problem often arises as to how much should the imagined scenery be consciously willed to happen and how much should it be allowed to flow without effort, for explorers often feel unsure of results that they have manipulated or caused to occur. There is a delicate balance to achieve here, for complete passivity will produce little or nothing, whereas conscious manipulation of the images that occur means that the ego is controlling and censoring everything that rises into its domain.

There is a trick involved then and, once this is recognised, the results should flow quite easily, unless a psychological block against using the imagination exists. It is necessary to provide the initial impulse, *but not to change anything once it has arisen or been created in the mind's eye*. Take whatever image is created first. The process is analogous to asking someone to paint a picture but giving the artist one opportunity only – the rules don't allow anything to be rubbed out or changed, for this is critical censorship by the ego.

In painting a real picture this would present a hampering limitation but on the inner journey this is not so, for the images can change, move and grow in their own way, or rather in the way that the unconscious directs. The conscious self should provide the initial push to get the ball rolling, and should help it when it gets stuck, *but should not control the direction in which the ball rolls.*

The appearance of an animal or bird at the next stage of the initial journey is another trick in order to lead the explorer deeper into the surrounding countryside to discover what secrets it may reveal. It might also interest you to know the symbolic associations that are usually made with the particular creature that happens to appear. For example, the owl is a symbol of wisdom, the raven is associated with fate, the fox with cunning, the horse with intellect and the dog with the Moon (itself a symbol of the unconscious and associated with Artemis or Diana). At this stage, guidance by an animal or bird represents the guidance of unconscious instinct, but this exploration needs to be done under the supervision of an entity associated with a much higher form of consciousness and hence the immediate introduction of the Guide figure.

The Guide in its most elementary form simply represents an embodiment of the explorer's own common sense and in its highest form is a symbol of wisdom, a wisdom born of vast experience, already held within, concerning the realm which the explorer is about to discover. This is an important and powerful symbol which may at first be difficult to visualise, partly because it may be the first conscious encounter of the explorer with a personified image, and secondly because the ego may present an unexpected block.

The ego doesn't like to think that there is anything more to itself than it is conscious of. When it gets an inkling that the explorer may be setting off to show that there is, it gets a bit upset and tries to devise ways of preventing the explorer from making any progress.

Ego blocks that I have encountered include insurmountable brick walls, frightening animals that try to deter the explorer and any amount of ingenious obstacles invented for the express purpose of barring the way to self-exploration. These include the possible appearance of a false guide and this can be detected in the manner indicated in the description of the initial journey (see page 50).

The way to deal with such obstacles in general is simply to give them no energy, to ignore them, walk straight through or past them. This sounds trite, but I've been surprised by the number of people who have had difficulty getting out of the cave because, for example, the exit is blocked by an immovable object.

There is a possibility that the blocking energy may indicate that it is wrong to explore further, because the use of the creative imagination is not right for the individual concerned. Common sense needs to be applied here, especially in the case of subjects who could have a weak ego, and are psychologically sensitive or unbalanced. If it feels wrong, don't do it.

In practice, I have found no cases where this is so, but it is as well to be aware of the possibility, as this technique could open up a pathway for the entry into consciousness of unwanted elements that are difficult to cope with. A person with no strong psychological problems has nothing to worry about.

If the imagining exercise is found difficult, even when conditions are conducive to it through a relaxed, comfortable atmosphere and state of being, this is probably because the explorer has become out of touch with the Fire element of his or her being, from which the imagination issues.

In some cases, I have found that the ego-block is followed by a state of slight depression after attempting the exercise, but this is also rare and transitory. This may occur because the ego tries to impress on the explorer that the exercises are to no avail. What's the use, he or she asks. Subsequently the explorer stops doing the exercises and the ego has won.

Take no notice, but try imposing a slight touch of discipline and pressure, for the ensuing results may be quite a vivid and remarkable experience.

Explorers often find difficulty in visualising any detail of the Guide's face. Don't worry if this is so, for time and familiarity will clarify the images, as the unconscious energies are transformed and allowed to flow more freely.

The astrological symbols are useful for picturing a personified form of the archetypal energies, and the explorer can now go into the relationships that exist between them. These symbols are used in the birth chart, which can now act as a map for the inner journey. For example, Saturn and Venus (or any other combination) can be visualised as people in order to discover how the two aspects of the psyche that they represent relate to one another. (For example, a birth chart may reveal them to be linked through a difficult tension, or conversely they may form an easy, flowing relationship.) Do they work well together, or is there a tension that needs somehow to be resolved?

Asking a personified image for a gift or symbol helps to solidify the relationship between the ego and the particular aspect of the psyche being dealt with. In the preliminary journey, the Sun was asked for a gift or symbol which the explorer could make use of. Meditation on the meaning of the symbol is useful, and also it can be watched with the mind's eye and allowed to change, evolve and become transformed in appearance. The gift of an apple, for example, which the Sun may have indicated represented the fruit of past experience, may break open revealing its seeds, which may germinate and begin to grow into a new tree (potentially a new experience).

When working on an exploration using the astrological symbols, it is necessary to realise that they often get mixed up. For example, Venus may appear with qualities that are more usually associated with the Moon. This may indicate aspects of the psyche that are insufficiently differentiated and are confused. The explorer should allow the personified symbols to change and evolve.

When these initial encounters with the planetary symbols have been experienced, the explorer should use his or her imagination in any way possible to widen the range of experience and go off exploring this new-found inner country, where no explorer has ever been before. But remember always to take the Guide along, for he or she can be invaluable in helping to clarify the significance of inner experiences.

The Guide will also help to deal with any tricky or enigmatic situations that may arise. Whenever I indicate this to an individual, it seems the first thing that he or she is bound to do is to find out what will happen when an exploration is undertaken *without* the Guide, and usually the answer is nothing. In this event, however, you only need to ask inwardly for the Guide to come and he or she will do so.

Try asking another person to act as a sort of outer guide, taking you through the inner journey. This can be a powerful combination. Usually the other person strikes up quite a relationship with the inner Guide whose form may then change and evolve. One person whom I worked with over a long period of time found that after a while a *second* guide appeared. This was at first disconcerting, for this second guide was very similar to the popular image of an angel, complete with golden wings.

The experience of the Guide bears some resemblance to a 'spirit guide', both being developments that can occur from the personification of common sense and wisdom. It matters not what name we use to label the Guide experience; the important thing is to recognise its *reality*. The use of the creative imagination in the way described does not create mere illusions, though this may be difficult to accept at first. The essential thing is to come to the realisation that there is a form of *inner reality*, of inner fact, *that does not exist until it is created* and this is the function of the imagination, to create a link between our normal three-dimensional, temporal reality and the non-temporal dimensions of the unconscious.

It is by no means necessary to employ the symbols of

astrology for the inner journey. The possibilities are limited only in as much as the imagination itself is limited – although a system such as astrology is extremely useful as a reference point and for identifying specific aspects of the personality. To help in this process, more information about the astrological symbols is given in Chapters 5 (houses), 6 (the zodiac) and 7 (the planets).

Ancient mythological tales can supply endless scenarios which the explorer can recreate. Participation in this sort of imaginative exercise can give tremendous insight into not only the nature of personality but even more so into the processes of the unconscious. Take, for example, the story from Greek mythology of Actaeon's surprise meeting one day with Artemis, goddess of the moon and virgin huntress, when he was in the woods hunting. Actaeon stumbled across Artemis while she was naked and bathing at her leisure. He was cruelly punished for spying on her at her toilet (he was turned into a stag which his own hounds devoured), a rather unfortunate end to the tale. But what would *your* reaction be if you were exploring a dark wood and chanced to enter a glade where a powerful and beautiful goddess was bathing in the moonlight? Or alternatively, as a woman taking the part of Artemis, how would you react if you were intruded upon in this situation?

All the time that the inner exploration is continuing, the explorer should put an emphasis on the way that inner experiences can be integrated and made use of in the course of everyday life. If the effect of an inner experience seems to be negative, common sense should be applied in deciding whether this is an aspect of the journey that needs to be faced and dealt with, or whether it should be rejected and dismissed so that any negative influences are dismissed along with it.

Because this approach to self-exploration is essentially a visual one, a knowledge of the significance and effects of different colours is useful, especially in the advanced stages when there may be an interest in the process of healing (the

Guide is often useful in demonstrating the use and effect of colour in this connection).

The visual approach by no means devalues or obviates the imaginative experience of sound or smell – the more sensory the experience, the more effective the results. If difficulty is found in obtaining any imaginative, physical–sensory experience, then the explorer should try to learn what is the most effective approach. Impressions of any kind are relevant, especially dialogue and feelings. For example, someone might describe his or her experience of the personified Sun in this manner: 'I couldn't exactly visualise the Sun as a person, but I felt that it was very tall and friendly towards me and was definitely a male. I got a warm, pleasant feeling when I tried to experience its presence, as if the Sun wanted to help me and fill me with warmth and love. A thought came to me at this time that perhaps I could fill myself with the Sun's warmth and then radiate it to others.'

Thoughts play a valid part in the process, and because of this it is a technique highly suitable for the Western mind – those who try the disciplined meditation techniques of the East usually find that the most difficult task is to still their thoughts.

At this point of the inner journey it becomes clear that religious revelation, divine guidance, psychic mediumship, channelling, exploration of past-life experiences, psychic healing and astral travel all stem from a contact with the inner worlds. These processes, even though they are little understood, can at least now be seen to have a basis which, if not rational, in the generally accepted sense, is at least reasonable enough for them to be taken seriously.

The experience of contacting and working with inner guidance is described fully by Edwin C. Steinbrecher[1] —

> It was during [the] initial arbitration phase that I experienced the difference between *ego* and *non-ego* elements in my own

---

1. Edwin C. Steinbrecher's *The Inner Guide Meditation* (Aquarian Press), is an invaluable source of further information about the technique that I have described.

psyche. My imagination took on a life of its own. Conflicting archetypal forms would not be pushed into agreement or easy reconciliations. Where I had supposed, 'I'm making most of this up,' I soon found experiences full of surprises. It became dramatically clear to me that these were *living* entities I was dealing with, and that my ego could not get them to co-operate or come together just because I thought they should or asked them to. They seemed to be separate, sometimes alien, entities totally unlike any familiar aspect of myself. They had their own likes and dislikes, interests and aversions, moods and temperaments. Their behaviours, as I observed and interacted with them, were often completely unpredictable. Occasionally they were hostile to me. Sometimes they totally ignored my presence, and only with the greatest effort could I attract their attention and get them to communicate with me. To get behaviour change or co-operation from them, *I* usually had to agree to make changes in my outer world, modify my behaviour or agree on new actions. They were most explicit about the changes they required from me or from my life in exchange for their co-operation or assistance.

As this inner process went on, I began to notice new phenomena occurring in my outer world. Those people in my life whom my ego regarded as negative or destructive began to change for the better or go out of my life. It seemed that everyone around me was suddenly beginning to 'get it together' as I continued to do the inner work.

To summarise, the patterns of inner growth can be experienced through dreams and the imagination, which forge a relationship between the everyday reality of life and the little explored inner dimensions of consciousness. And what a valuable relationship it is. To have the unconscious as an ally is to have the whole force of nature with one. No longer acting as an isolated person, one can experience and work with the unfolding patterns of life.

The remainder of this book will deal specifically with astrological symbolism, as the reader will now be able to see how this can be used in exploring inner space. Knowledge of the basic symbolism associated with astrology will be of assistance in the meditation and visualisation technique that I have described, for exploring and interpreting the inner images that arise. Traditional astrologers will also find much of value in adding to their understanding of the signs of the zodiac, planets and their cycles, and the astrological houses.

We have seen how symbols can stem from within, manifesting through dreams and the imagination, or occur in systems such as astrology that chart the whole domain of human personality and growth. Astrology presents this in terms of the cycles and patterns associated with the planets and signs of the zodiac. We only need to clothe these symbols with our own personal projections to be ready to see how astrology can be used as a mirror in which to view these aspects of ourselves, our hopes, wishes, fears, ambitions, successes and failures. Astrology becomes then a tool, not so much for predicting the future as for reflecting back an image of the whole person and his or her unfolding life cycles.

CHAPTER 3

THE LANGUAGE OF ASTROLOGY

Astrology has developed from an ancient and now somewhat outmoded system of prediction to a modern means of exploring the inner worlds. The birth chart is a map of the inner universe, describing patterns of psychological growth and which contains symbols that reveal unconscious dimensions within ourselves.

The astrological birth chart is a map of the zodiac and the planets set up for the time and place of birth of the individual to whom it refers. The zodiac is a belt in the heavens extending about 8° on each side of the path followed by the sun and containing the path of the planets. It is divided into 12 equal sectors known as the signs. Each sign therefore measures 30° and is named after one of the constellations. The signs and constellations do not coincide, though they slightly overlap.

The birth chart is usually drawn in the form of a circle, which is of course a symbol of wholeness. The glyphs for the signs appear round the circumference of the birth chart. The order in which they appear corresponds with that of the signs through which the sun progresses in its apparent journey around the earth during its yearly cycle. For example, the sun is said to enter the sign of Aries at the spring equinox, then it progresses into Taurus, Gemini, Cancer, Leo, Virgo, Libra, Scorpio, Sagittarius, Capricorn, Aquarius and Pisces, and it again enters Aries at the next spring equinox to begin a new cycle. Seen from the earth, all the planets and the sun and moon move at varying speeds through the zodiac. Within the circle of the birth chart lie all possibilities for the individual it refers to and it will reflect not only conscious features of the self but the unconscious too, i.e. it will reflect the whole individual, and all that he or she may become. It is the task of the person to whom the birth chart refers to relate to his symbols, not for the symbols to relate to him. The answers to our questions come from within; the symbols of astrology simply point to where the answers lie.

Each sign of the zodiac represents a particular manner, or mode of operation, or 'influence'. For example, any planet positioned in Aries will come under the influence of Aries and its symbolic energy will be modified in the appropriate manner by the Aries type of influence.

The signs can be divided into four groups known as the elements or 'triplicities': Fire, Air, Earth and Water. There are three signs of the zodiac belonging to each of the triplicities.

The signs can also be divided in a different way, into three groups known as the qualities or 'quadruplicities': Cardinal, Fixed and Mutable. There are four signs of the zodiac in each of the quadruplicities.

The signs can also be divided in another way, into two groups, known as either positive or negative (masculine and feminine would be better words to use, for 'negative' implies 'bad' and here this is not the case).

Each sign will fall into one of the categories of elements, one of the qualities, and will either be positive or negative. Reference to the table below should make this clearer. For example, Aries is Cardinal Fire, and is a positive sign. Also refer to the wheel in Fig. 1, which gives a basic description of each zodiac sign and its associated symbol. For example, Sagittarius is a positive, Mutable, Fire sign and, from the table, the associated key words are: adaptable, variable (Mutable) and energetic, assertive (Fire).

These key words are useful in forming a basis for estab-

ELEMENTS			QUALITIES		
FIRE	ENERGETIC ASSERTIVE		CARDINAL	ENTERPRISING INITIATING	
AIR	COMMUNICATIVE MENTALLY ACTIVE		FIXED	INTENSE STEADFAST	
EARTH	PRACTICAL RESTRAINED				
WATER	EMOTIONAL INTUITIVE		MUTABLE	ADAPTABLE VARIABLE	
MASCULINE PRINCIPLE			SELF-EXPRESSIVE; SPONTANEOUS; EXTROVERT		
FEMININE PRINCIPLE			SELF-REPRESSIVE; RECEPTIVE; INTROVERT		

lishing the fuller meaning of each sign which the reader can develop through further reading and experience.

Each of the planets, including the sun and moon, is associated with a particular type of energy or principle of operation. For example, the sun represents the self, the source of the creative life force, and its position in the birth chart indicates the individual's life purpose. The following key shows the symbols of the planets and the energy or principle associated with each of them. For example, Jupiter represents 'expansion', meaning growth and development, especially through learning and experience.

Key

SUN	☉	THE SELF
MOON	☽	FEELINGS
MERCURY	☿	COMMUNICATION
VENUS	♀	RELATIONSHIP
MARS	♂	MOTIVATION
JUPITER	♃	EXPANSION

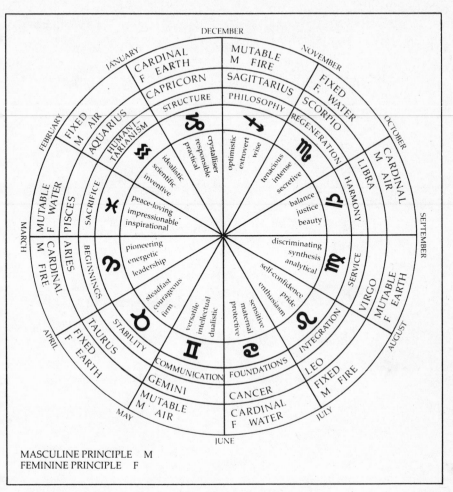

Fig. 1. Signs, keywords and concepts

SATURN	♄	LIMITATION
URANUS	♅	CHALLENGE
NEPTUNE	♆	IMAGINATION
PLUTO	♇	REGENERATION

65

The principle or nature of a planet will act through the signs as follows:

Through ♈ Aries — urgently, forcefully

♉ Taurus — productively, enduringly

♊ Gemini — adaptably, variably

♋ Cancer — defensively, nurturingly

♌ Leo — powerfully, creatively

♍ Virgo — analytically, critically

♎ Libra — relatedly, harmoniously

♏ Scorpio — penetratingly, intensely

♐ Sagittarius — extensively, freely

♑ Capricorn — traditionally, prudently

♒ Aquarius — unconventionally, sociably

♓ Pisces — nebulously, impressionably

For example, if in a birth chart Jupiter is positioned in the sign of Aries, then the principle of expansion is modified by Aries, i.e. in an urgent, forceful manner.

Fig. 2 also shows how a planet will act in each sign. This wheel shows which sign each planet rules, i.e. the one for which it has the closest affinity. When positioned in its own sign, the planet is said to be in dignity.

When the circle of the birth chart is drawn, it may be divided into 12 segments forming what are called the 12

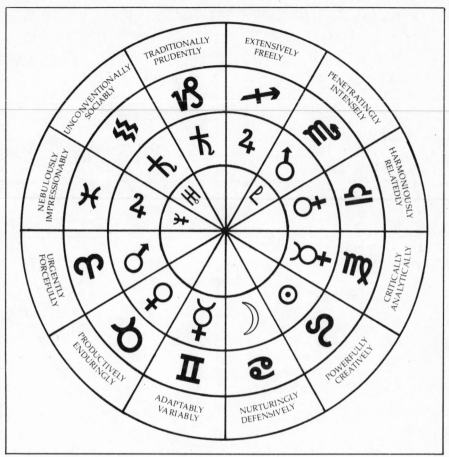

Fig. 2 *Ruling planets – operative principles. Three signs of the zodiac have two ruling planets, as shown*

'houses'. The wheel in Fig. 3 on page 68, shows how each of the 12 houses represents a particular area of life.

We now have three considerations to link together when interpreting a birth chart: the planets, which represent a particular archetypal energy; the signs which show how that energy will operate or be modified; and the houses which show in which area of life a particular energy will manifest itself. For example, if Mars is found to be positioned in Capricorn and the fourth house we can say: 'The

67

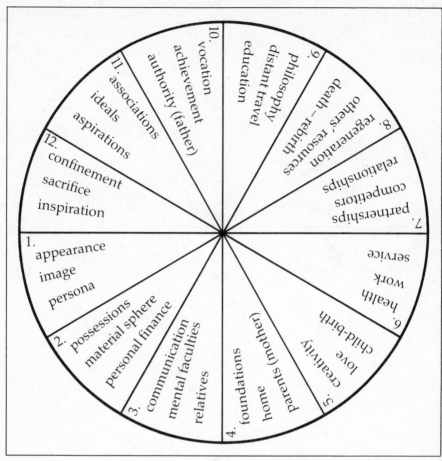

Fig. 3. The houses

physical, driving activity of Mars will be modified in a structured, prudent manner, especially in the area of home life.'

When two planets form a particular angular relationship with one another, they are said to form an 'aspect' and when this occurs the energies of the two planets link together. Some of the aspects are known to be difficult ones, representing a conflict or tension, and other aspects are known to be easy or flowing, in which case the two planets function well together and represent natural abilities. For

example, if in the birth chart Jupiter is in opposition to (180°
away from) Mercury, a difficult aspect, then expansion and
growth (Jupiter) will tend to 'oppose' communication (Mercury).

If you have your own birth chart, the keyword system can
be used to give a preliminary interpretation. Here are two
examples.

The sun is positioned in Aries and the fifth house. Inserting the keywords we can say: 'The life-giving energy of the
self (sun) operates in an urgent, forceful, pioneering, outgoing manner (through Aries) in the area of life related to
creativity and self-expression (fifth house).'

This keyword sentence can now be put into more meaningful language. For example, we could say: 'The basic life
energy or purpose of the individual will act in a forthright,
dynamic manner and will be directed towards a form of
creative self-expression, perhaps in the field of the arts or
theatre.'

Take as another example Mars positioned in Capricorn
and in the second house. Inserting the keywords, we can
say: 'The physical drive and motivation of the individual
(Mars) act in a structured, restrained, prudent manner
(through Capricorn) in the area of life related to material
concerns (second house). This would represent an individual
who strives towards material gain or has an urge towards
the understanding of material gain and the meaning of
possessions.'

Each planet in a birth chart can be considered in turn,
applying the keyword interpretations. To gain insight
through astrology, it is not even necessary to know the
details of interpretation techniques, although a deep study
of the subject can be rewarding. I believe that the astrologer
who uses the birth chart for detailed personal analysis has
had his day, for we are now learning that the true interpretation of these 'chance' configurations comes from an inner
process of the imagination and not from an outer academic
study of causes and effects. Through this attitude, individ-

69

uals can take responsibility for their own destiny, rather than believing it to be thrust upon them by presumed vibrations from Venus or Mars.

The foundation of the 'new astrology', therefore, is the forming of a *complete* picture of the nature of reality. Before considering the nature of the cycles and patterns that the planets, signs of the zodiac and astrological houses reveal to us, we should consider first in more detail some of the basic qualities that astrology encompasses through the polarity of the signs and their division into elements and qualities.

Polarity means the possession of contrasted or opposite qualities, principles or tendencies. Symbols are polar by nature. Thus when considering a property of any symbol, we should be aware that its opposite meaning is always possible, and hence great care must be taken for, like Janus, symbols are never entirely as they appear to be. For example, consider a symbol that represents creativity. This is a quality attributed to the zodiacal sign Leo. Now Leo can show either of two faces: one that can produce works of art and self-expression that have depth and beauty and in which great pride may be taken; or one in which creative expression may become self-centred. Self-aggrandisement and pride in the latter case come before the fall. The symbolism inherent in Leo shows that it can work either in a constructive or destructive manner and there is a subtle difference that separates these two faces of pride, represented by the Lion.

The zodiac is contained within a circle so that each sign faces another diametrically opposite to it and six pairs of opposite signs can be examined together. When this is done, they are also found to be polar opposites. Aries is diametrically opposite Libra and so on. Aries represents individuality, Libra represents relationship. The same pattern can be seen in operation in each of the other five pairs of signs.

One way to look at these relationships is to regard the opposite sign as possessing qualities which the other sign

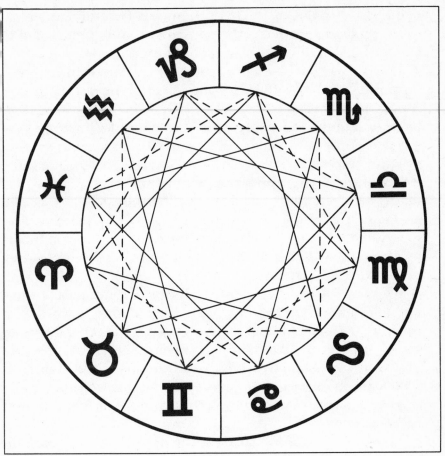

Fig. 4. Patterns in the zodiac

needs in order to achieve a balance, wholeness and completeness. For example, the individual Aries type needs to be able to relate with others in order not to suffer from isolation and, conversely, the Libran type of personality, that identifies itself through relationships, needs to be able to identify also the unique characteristics of individuality, in order to achieve personal independence.

An over-emphasis of one type of personality to the detriment of its polar opposite is not a psychologically healthy

71

condition. What is needed is a balance between the qualities of the polar opposites. This particular 'wholesome' quality expressed by the zodiac is repeated in many ways.

When two characteristics seem to be totally contrary and 'opposite' to each other, in other words are polar to each other, usually each is respectively denoted either as masculine (outgoing and expressive) or feminine (ingoing and receptive), or as positive and negative. Any energy flow, whether physical, mental or emotional, can be said to be either of these two opposites. So whenever a comparison is made between two qualities they become relative to one another and we must distinguish which is positive and masculine, or negative and feminine, by a convention that is established by common agreement. Note here that negative does not necessarily mean bad.

We view the physical world in terms of relative quantities and qualities. For example, we may define a particular direction as forwards and from this deduce that the opposite direction must be backwards. Forwards is not an absolute direction but a relative one, and our lives are organised according to relative definitions such as this, so that we can orientate ourselves, our thoughts, purposes, actions and achievements.

An expression of the polar nature of the zodiac is found in the designation of the signs as either masculine or feminine, and these are arrayed around the circle in an alternate manner: Aries, masculine; Taurus, feminine; Gemini, masculine; Cancer, feminine, and so on.

The zodiac contains within it many properties expressing the divisive nature with which we regard ourselves, but remember that its complete form is that of a circle, a symbol of wholeness – and of the Self.

The planets may also be regarded as either masculine or feminine in nature; they may each be considered to have properties that are associated with either the maleness of a man or the femaleness of a woman.

If a man is considered as a whole, like a symbol, he must

embody in some aspect of his nature the feminine qualities that balance the outward conscious nature. Jung called this particular polar opposite the 'anima'. Similarly, a woman must encompass the qualities of masculinity that can balance the outward conscious female nature and this hidden aspect of the female is called the 'animus'. In recognising these inner, polar opposite qualities, it becomes possible to make a psychological interpretation of the alchemical descriptions of the processes involved in a 'divine marriage'. This represents the union of opposites within the human psyche and results in a union or direct relationship between the inner and outer worlds of experience.

To reconcile any tension that exists between two energies or forces, whether physical, psychological or whatever, it is necessary to introduce a third factor, or force, which will put the two opposing forces in a condition of balance.

In mathematics, when calculating the exact dimensions of the third force, the two forces that are under consideration are represented in magnitude and direction by the two sides of a triangle. The dimensions of the balancing third force is proportional to the third side of the triangle. Thus we have what is called a *triangle of forces* and this idea gives an insight into the nature of the triangle as a symbol for the balancing of polar forces on a psychological level.

When dealing with psychological conflicts, the third or resolving factor is always discovered on a different plane to the conflicting problems. This means that in order to resolve a conflict, say between two points of view, it is necessary to be able to step outside the situation in order to obtain an objective solution which will resolve the conflict in a manner that encompasses both sides.

This is not the same as a compromise. It is a solution that puts the opposing forces in a state of dynamic balance. That is, they are still under tension but are in balance so that together they act in a complete or whole manner, and complement rather than oppose one another – they are married.

Hence, the next stage after the process of division into two is the introduction of a third, harmonising factor that completes the triangle of forces, ensures that polar forces complement rather than oppose and which instigates a state of dynamic tension which is necessary, on a psychological level, for the release of creative energy.

As an example of keeping psychological energies in balance, consider the case of the business person, who leads a highly active, stimulating mental life, but who takes little physical exercise. When the relationship between mind and body is lacking in balance like this, the body soon rebels with aches and pains, and if the cause of these psychosomatic disorders continues to be ignored then more serious complaints follow.

The psychic energies will also be unhealthily out of balance if the polar opposite qualities of the personality have no relationship. I once had an employer who, at work, was extremely aggressive and domineering. It came as a shock to meet him with his wife who treated him like a little boy. He had responded to this split between the worlds of home and work by becoming a 'Jekyll and Hyde'. When there is no relationship between the two extremes of personality within an individual, each tends to become an exaggerated caricature, with no further potential for growth or change.

The threefold nature of the psyche is recognised in most religious or spiritual approaches to the nature of reality. For example, the trinity of Father, Son and Holy Ghost in the Christian religion is well known in the Western world as a symbol of the threefold nature, reflected in the corresponding trinity of spirit, body and soul. Rudolf Steiner's works are based on the threefold nature of being which he considers as analogous to the realms of intellect, feeling and will. In this approach, the contemplative, dualistic mind (intellect) is polar and complementary to activity and expression (will), these two being dynamically balanced by value judgement and awareness of absolute qualities (feeling).

74

An expression of the trinity is found also in the symbols of astrology, whereby the 12 signs of the zodiac are divided into Cardinal, Fixed and Mutable, the quadruplicities introduced earlier in this chapter. Aries, Libra, Cancer and Capricorn are called Cardinal; Leo, Aquarius, Taurus and Scorpio are the Fixed signs; Sagittarius, Gemini, Virgo and Pisces are Mutable.

The 12 archetypal energies that are symbolised by the signs of the zodiac have three characteristic modes of expression. *Cardinal* indicates a form whereby energy is *generated* and converted and is perhaps analogous to the generation of electrical energy from the circular movement of the wheel. The energy is already there in the movement of the wheel, but it may be converted and generated in a more useful form by the Cardinal mode of archetypal expression.

Fixed indicates a form whereby the energy content of the archetype is *concentrated*, or given a particular direction, or is focused at a particular point. *Mutable*, on the other hand, indicates a form of energy that is *distributed* in all directions. As a threefold expression of the nature of consciousness, the Mutable and Cardinal archetypes are polar in nature with the Fixed action providing the dynamic balancing factor.

If the signs of the zodiac belonging to one of the quadruplicities (say all the Cardinal signs) are linked together with imaginary straight lines in the circle of the zodiac, they will be found to be positioned each at the corner of a square (see Fig. 4, p. 71). Thus there are four groups of the three forms of expression. These four correspond with the elements of nature, and are termed Fire, Air, Earth and Water, as described earlier.

The element Fire is expressed as force, drive, passion. Air is expressed in the intellect, Water is expressed in emotion, and Earth as physical energy and all things tangible. Fire and Air are masculine, positive elements, whereas Water and Earth are female, or negative elements.

The square, which represents the four elements, is a symbol of earthly fulfilment. The four archangels of the Christian mythos are often represented pictorially as a lion (Michael), an eagle (Gabriel), a bull or calf (Uriel) and a man (Raphael), corresponding to the elements Fire, Air, Earth and Water respectively.

Thus the content of the archetypes is channelled in three ways, and the form in which they are expressed is made up of the four elements, each expressing a basic kind of manifested, detectable energy.

The four elements correspond to any quaternity that forms an expression of wholeness. For example, science, philosophy, art and religion correspond to Air, Fire, Earth and Water respectively. Science and philosophy are positive, rational, outward-looking methods of understanding and experiencing reality, whereas art and religion possess a negative, inward, non-rational view. All are needed to form a complete picture.

In particular, the four astrological elements are helpful in understanding the psychological types that have been defined by depth psychology and which are classified into the thinking, feeling, sensing and intuitive types of personality. Feeling here includes the ability to make value judgements as well as emotional sensitivity, and intuition is defined as the ability to see future possibilities without recourse to conscious reasoning. Sensing indicates reliance on the physical senses.

A person who uses one of these faculties, or 'functions', to a much greater extent than any of the other three as a means of gaining and assessing experience is classified in this system accordingly. For example, an intellectual would be classified as a thinking type, but obviously this is a gross over-simplification for, like the four elements, these four functions are present in varying degrees of conscious use. Thinking and feeling are considered as polar opposite, rational functions, both under the control of the individual. Sensing and intuition are likewise polar opposites, but they are non-rational functions that happen *to* the individual.

Depth psychology has gone one step further than this by establishing that if a function is predominant and has been consciously well developed by the individual then the polar opposite will be correspondingly influential, but will operate unconsciously. This is called the 'inferior' function.

The inferior function will often be compensated for in such a way that a person will be drawn to form a relationship that provides the missing factor through attraction to another whose dominant function is the same as that of his or her inferior function. For example, a thinking type may discover the hidden aspect of his or her personality by forming a relationship with a feeling type. If this process of compensation does not occur, then like usually attracts like. The rule is that any content of the psyche which remains unconscious will be projected into the realm of outer experience.

The inferior functions are described as being undifferentiated, for they are not sufficiently integrated into the field of conscious awareness and cannot be used to make valid judgements of experience. They remain primitive and undeveloped and as they operate unconsciously can easily control, or at least dominate, an individual who remains unaware of this naive, immature aspect of his or her personality.

As an example of inferior feelings in a thinking type, Marie-Louise von Franz says[1] —

> Outwardly the extroverted thinking type does not give the impression of having strong feelings. In a politician, the inferior function might unconsciously manifest itself in a deep-rooted and steadfast loyalty to his country. But it might also induce him to drop an atom bomb or commit some other destructive act. Unconscious and undeveloped feeling is barbaric and absolute, and therefore sometimes hidden destructive fanaticism suddenly bursts out of the extroverted thinking type. These people are incapable of seeing that, from a feeling standard, other people might have another value, for they do not question the inner

---

1. *Jung's Typology* (Spring Publications).

values which they defend . . . These hidden introverted feelings of the extroverted thinking type are sometimes very childish. After the death of such people one sometimes finds notebooks in which childish poems have been written to a far-away woman whom they have never met in their lives and in which a lot of sentimental, mystical feeling is poured out.

The four elements have been equated with the four psychological types as: Fire, intuition; Air, thinking; Earth, sensing; and Water, feeling. This is a useful comparison and it can be seen how a predominance of a particular element can be associated with a psychological type.

Intuition does not quite fit from the point of view of astrological symbolism. It is more useful and meaningful to equate Fire with the imagination, rather than intuition, and what might be called in psychological parlance an 'imaginative type'. It is easier to identify a type of person who lives in his thoughts, or feelings, or sensations, or in his imagination, and not so easy to identify the type of person who lives in his intuitions, or who identifies closely with them.

In the education system of our modern culture, emphasis is placed on the value of the Air element, often to the detriment of the other three, especially the non-rational functions of sensing and imagination (or intuition) and it can be seen how this is not a healthy state of affairs. It is akin to trying to understand the nature of reality by rational methods alone. It is necessary to give equal value to each of the four elements and to become conscious of their individual significance so that they may be integrated to form a functioning whole and healthy personality. The meditation exercises in the previous chapter describe a manner in which the Fire element can be developed, experienced and integrated, for the imagination plays a vital role as a mediator between the conscious self and the inner dimensions of the unconscious.

Having obtained an insight into the nature of astrological symbolism and the human personality that it seeks to describe, it is now possible to consider the meaning of the

Fig. 5   The four elements and the corresponding four psychological types

different cycles and patterns that astrology presents to us. This will be the subject of the remaining chapters, beginning with the fundamental cycle, as exemplified by the phases of the moon.

CHAPTER 4
PHASES OF THE MOON

The fundamental life cycle is described by the consecutive phases
of the moon, from birth at new moon, through the crisis times of
the quarter phases, to fulfilment or failure at the full moon.
Eight phases in all are identified.

All the events that we can observe in the world that surrounds us are contained within an underlying pattern that is
cyclic in nature.

Anything that exists can be observed to follow the underlying archetypal pattern of birth, growth, death and rebirth
– even the modern creation theory about how the universe
came into being follows this archetypal pattern. This theory
is that matter condensed, or folded in on itself to such a high
degree of energetic intensity that it caused a nuclear reaction
of such force that the original matter of the universe was
blown outwards into space in countless fragments, of which
our earth is but one. All the fragments are now travelling away
from the point of the original explosion (the 'big bang').

At some time in the distant future, the relative velocities
of the fragments (stars, planets, galaxies, etc.) hurtling
through space may be insufficient to counteract the gravi-
tational forces acting between them and they will then tend
to be drawn back towards one another, to collapse in on one
another again, forming, as in the beginning, a single mass.
The universe at such a time, metaphorically speaking, will

die.[1] But the process will go on, for again the imploding forces will spark off a thermal nuclear chain reaction including the next 'big bang' and birth of a new universe.

The idea of a periodically expanding and contracting universe formed the central theme of ancient Indian cosmologies, which described the universe as organic and rhythmically moving. The Hindus developed evolutionary cosmologies which came very close to our modern scientific models.

Even on the largest scale imaginable, there is a cyclic process at work that moves from birth, to death, to rebirth, and this archetypal process can be seen at work in any event, whether it is the life of a planet, a country, a civilisation, a group of people or an individual animal, flower or human being.

Individual events occurring within the symmetrical pattern of the archetypal cycle are often related to it, but are not dependent on it. For example, there is the daily cycle which corresponds to the rotation of the earth about its own axis. This cycle is repeated every 24 hours, but the events which occur within this cycle are not necessarily repeated, although some *tend* to be. For instance, we tend to wake up in the morning, work during the day and sleep at night. This process is related to the daily cycle, so that our lives may fit in and flow with it, although we are not impelled to do so. This is the case with all archetypal cycles which form a backdrop against which specific events are acted out. The implication of this is that the stars and planets should not be allowed to rule us but should act as our guides. They can only play this role if we make a *conscious* link between their life patterns and those of our own.

In psychological terms, if there is an unconscious cycle of

---

1. The so called 'big crunch'. We cannot know what happened before the original big bang because, according to this particular theory, this is the point at which time began, an idea that many people do not like because it implies divine intervention. Refer to Stephen Hawking's *A Brief History of Time* (Bantam) for a description of the possible alternatives.

growth or development within the psyche then it will tend to be projected onto a suitable hook in the outside world. For example, a 29-year inner cycle could be projected onto the planet Saturn, whose orbit is approximately of 29 years' duration. A monthly cycle could be attributed to the phases of the moon which complete one cycle every $29\frac{1}{2}$ days.

Within each cycle can be discovered other cycles and within these even more, so, from the original archetypal cycle, the picture becomes more complex – but all of these complex cycles and their interrelationships can be based on that one archetype which is the original meaning of the cycle.

Astrology is a study of the complex interrelationships of all the different cycles that can be observed at work within the history of humankind and our environment. Each cycle of mental, emotional and physical growth may be related to the symbolic function and rhythm of a planet in the solar system. The study of these cyclic relationships has further helped to show how they are all interrelated, how one cycle depends on and affects all the rest.

The basic nature of the cycle can be described by the relationship that exists in the heavens between the sun and the moon. This, called the *lunation cycle*, the time between successive new moons, represents different stages, or phases, of the basic cyclic pattern of unfoldment of life on earth. The lunation cycle is the shortest planetary cycle of relationships that is observable within our solar system, which is why astrologers have used it to describe the basis of all cycles.[2]

Before illustrating the significance of each phase within the lunation cycle as it unfolds its story each month, it is necessary to make an important distinction. The phases of the moon represent a cycle of relationship between the sun

---

2. In Dane Rudhyar's *The Lunation Cycle* (Aurora Press), the author is to be credited with the first full description of the astrological interpretation of the moon's phases in relation to the individual birth chart, the phase shown at the time of birth representing the 'phase' reached by the individual in his or her evolution.

and moon which begins at the new moon when the sun and moon are coincident (conjunct) when viewed from the earth, and ends at the next new moon, approximately $29\frac{1}{2}$ days later, when they are again conjunct. Now the orbit of the moon around the earth is actually about $27\frac{1}{2}$ days, but because we are considering its position in relation to the sun and because the sun is also (apparently) moving around the earth, the moon moves slightly more than one complete circle before it again meets, or conjuncts, the sun.

The cycle of relationship between the sun and moon is divided into eight phases. Although the basic cycle could theoretically be divided into any number, the division by eight easily identifies each stage of the moon's waxing and waning as we observe it from the earth. The number eight also symbolises the aim of achieving concrete results that are of direct value and use. The symbolic significance that can be attached to each of the eight phases of the moon within the lunation cycle is shown in Fig. 6 on page 84.

New moon

This occurs when the moon and the sun are on the same side of the earth and exactly aligned, with the moon between the sun and the earth. As none of the life-giving light emanations of the sun can reach the earth at the beginning of the new moon phase, we are unable to see the moon in the night sky. It is the beginning of the cycle, at the point where the new life is about to emerge.

The new moon phase lasts until the moon is advanced 45° ahead of the sun (each phase lasts just under four days) and this phase of the cycle represents the beginning or emergence of life in every sense. All experience symbolised here is new and undifferentiated, and the individual at the new moon phase has no past experience on which to draw, but views all the world as undifferentiated from the self (or from itself, if we were dealing with a system other than a human one). All that the individual can do at this stage is to accept

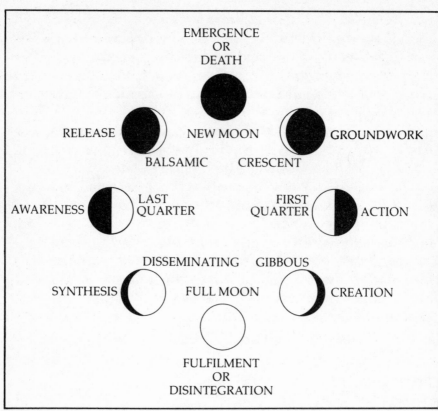

Fig. 6 *The cycle of life, represented by the lunation cycle. Each phase of the cycle has been given a characteristic meaning*

the experience of its own emergence as fully and as openly as possible. It is impossible for any organism at the new moon phase of experience to pass any form of judgement for there is as yet no apparent existence of pre-established criteria on which to base the judgement. All that the individual can do is accept his or her new existence, and that he or she has taken the first step along a path that leads back to its beginning, hopefully one step up the spiral of evolution.

Crescent

This occurs when the moon is 45°–90° ahead of the sun and represents the stage at which the organism needs to establish itself and its future purpose. This means turning briefly towards the past and the previous cycle so that firm roots can be established that draw nourishment from past achievements. It is necessary here for the individual both to recognise the link with the past *and* to assert his or her own individuality. The groundwork is here being laid for future growth, fruit and harvest, and this groundwork must be based on firm foundations. Hence this phase represents a certain amount of consideration for the past, but with a purpose whose aim is definitely future-orientated.

It is necessary for any work of importance, whether it be the development of a human being, or even of a civilisation, to learn from the past and put that accumulation of wisdom to good use. So at the crescent phase of existence the individual begins to realise that all he or she is today is because of all they have been in the past. The strength and purpose of the roots put down here mark the manner in which future growth is to be manifest.

First quarter

The first quarter phase occurs when the moon is 90°–135° ahead of the sun and represents a desire for action. It is symbolic of the adolescent phase of life where the individual has no sensitivity towards the deeper or long-term consequences of action but simply wants to go ahead and get on with the job in hand, the task that was established during the previous phase. This phase symbolises the active, positive, forthright phase of existence which is still uncomplicated by an awareness that extends beyond the immediate field of perception. This is the time where growth is witnessed at its most rapid and, because there is no growth without pain or suffering (especially psychological growth), this is the phase where pain is first experienced as a reality and it can come as a shock, for it is realised through this shock that others must experience pain too. At the beginning of the phase, the individual was unaware of anything but the desire to act. Now, towards the end of the phase, the consequences inherent in the action are perceived.

Gibbous

When the moon is almost full, it is said to be at the gibbous phase and this occurs when the moon is 135°–180° ahead of the sun, beginning just under four days before the full moon. Because the individual or organism has now reached the stage of awareness that actions have consequences which echo through all levels of being, self-expression becomes imperative: 'Look what I am doing, how important and clever I am.' This can indicate a strong enough will to create works of art of inspiring beauty, or we may find here the seeds of undoing hidden in the burgeoning strength of a self-centred ego.

At this phase, if all goes well, the individual recognises that true creation lies outside his or her powers and that the individual only acts as a channel for the creative process. Because of this, the need for perfection of the channel is recognised so that perfection of creation may be achieved at this stage; the system, organism or individual approaches its peak – a civilisation brings forth new criteria of perfection in all fields of endeavour, the individual becomes a master craftsperson and the flower holds forth its perfectly formed bud ready to receive the sun's rays and open in celebration of its achievements.

So the emphasis of this phase of life is on self-expression in full awareness of the consequences of past actions and the current opening to the flow of creation, which begins to approach its culmination. The vehicle for the perfect creative process is achieved during this phase. Now, however, the motivation of the individual must be reassessed. At the new moon phase the individual had pure purpose, with no criteria available to judge it. But now the consciousness of individuality has been established and with it the need to determine questions of morality and the conscious acceptance of acting in the name of Light or Darkness.

If the Light is chosen, based on humanitarian principles, the creativity of the individual will flower in the next phase of unfoldment. If the choice is Darkness, based on egocentric ideas of self-aggrandisement, this creativity will be turned head over heels into a careering force of self-destruction.

Full moon

We are now half-way through the lunation cycle and this phase occurs when sun and moon are aligned on opposite sides of the earth so that the face of the moon is fully exposed to reflect the sun's rays to earth. The full moon phase occurs when the moon is 180°–225° away from the sun and we can see in the sky the full face of the moon.

Two possibilities are inherent in this phase which depend on the conscious choice of the individual during the previous phase, i.e. during the gibbous phase. If the motivation has been in the name of Light, then the flower opens, the civilisation enters a Golden Age, the man or woman achieves a life-long ambition. All that has gone before culminates during this phase and attains the maximum possible achievement defined so long ago by the seed that germinated or was born at the new moon phase.

All that has been learnt may be put to use; all that has been worked for becomes manifest as reward. The full moon symbolises a period of fruition and culmination. It is important not to limit an aim unnecessarily, for that aim is reached at the full moon phase in the cycle of life.

The full moon may, however, bring about a collapse and total disintegration of all that has been worked for. This is the second of the possibilities here and, because there is this uncertainty and so much at stake, the beginning of the phase, at the exact full moon, is a time of great tension and expectancy. The sun and moon on opposite sides of the earth are in opposition to one another with the earth caught right in the middle.

If the purpose and motivation established during the gibbous phase has been in the name of Darkness, then the flower withers through lack of sustaining nourishment and care; the civilisation crumbles into disorder, immorality and a Dark Age; the man or woman suffers psychic attack and defeat from the very forces that he or she hoped to control.

The full moon emphasises the dual nature of all that is. Two possibilities are shown here at the culmination of the cycle before it enters on the path of return that leads to the next new moon: achievement or decay. Whatever the result, the cycle must continue to the next phase.

Disseminating

This phase occurs when the moon is 225°–270° ahead of the sun and is, so to speak, approaching it from the other side. The full moon phase sees the turning point at which the individual begins to head for home again. What is there left after the fullness of achievement? The answer lies in the future and the disseminating phase represents the time in the cycle when it is realised that there will be a future and that now is the time to try and discover how all the achievements of the past may be synthesised in such a way that their value is not transitory, but can have a lasting meaning.

Still tied to his or her achievements, the individual tries now to view them in a wider context, to see how the achievements and flowering of others can be synthesised to form a whole.

If disintegration occurred during the full moon phase of the cycle, then it is now necessary to pick up the bits, to sew the pieces back together and forge a way into the future in expectancy of the beginning of a new cycle. The emphasis is on a synthesising of all that the person is conscious of, so that some meaning can be made from it, a meaning that goes beyond the normal bounds of experience. This indicates the presence of dissatisfaction, for now the limit has been reached. The individual who now recognises the reality of infinity sees that the limit could have been established higher, further; human nature embodies this restless perpetual striving for perfection. The dissatisfaction inherent in the synthesising aspect of the disseminating phase lends the impetus to take the individual onwards into the unknown future.

Third quarter

The moon during this phase is 270°–315° ahead of the sun. Here the end of the cycle is sensed as a reality for the first time; the individual is asked to face death. This is done in the light of the knowledge that death does not indicate the end but a new beginning, and with this realisation comes a great urgency to prepare for this future life. The individual must relinquish the past and its achievements ('you can't take it with you') and prepare the groundwork for the future life. As a reincarnating individual, the next life-span is determined by the actions, decisions and achievements of the previous incarnation, and at the third quarter phase it is found to be necessary to reorient the whole of the current life span so that its aim is now the future itself. The individual relinquishes a hold on all that has been achieved so that this may now be adopted and used for the benefit of mankind as a whole – there are those younger, with more enthusiasm and drive coming up from below and a place must be made for them. This is perhaps the most difficult stage to pass through, for the individual is asked to let go of all that he or she has been, to let go, with no concrete image in view of what the future holds in store. So reorientation here must be an act of faith and that is one of the most difficult lessons of all.

Balsamic

We now enter the last phase in the archetypal cycle of life represented by the moon's phases. The moon is now

315°–360° ahead of the sun and close to an exact conjunction once again when the new moon is at 360° of the current cycle, or 0°, the beginning of the next.

The final phase represents a time of great release, when all the tools that have been used and stretched to the full over the period of this cycle have become tired and worn out and approach the limit of their allotted life-span. The organism or individual turns at this point away from the realm of the limited and finite aspects of nature to those that are infinite and beyond the realms of normal perception. It is now a great relief to have no choice and yet to know that in the removal of that choice of life or death lie the infinite possibilities of the future. The last phase in any life span is the most difficult on which to pass any objective judgement, for we are still in the current cycle whereas the individual concerned is about to pass out of it, enter into the reality of infinity and go we know not where.

On all sides there have been limitations, duty and lessons that are relevant to the current cycle. Now they are in the past and the individual may return to the place from whence he or she came. The end is the beginning. The end is the new moon and the beginning is the new moon.

It is illogical and even ludicrous that birth should be regarded as something appearing out of nothing. Rather it would make more sense to view this process as something manifesting out of everything for a purpose and for a particular period of time represented by the archetypal description of the lunation cycle. At death the individual simply returns back to everything – in other words, back to the point from which he or she started, thus closing the circle into an infinitely continuous loop.

* * *

There are certain crises or turning points marked out at specific times in the lunation cycle. These occur at the new moon, the first quarter, full moon and the last quarter. The crisis points of the new and full moons should be clear from the foregoing descriptions of the phases, but it is probably not quite so clear why the quarter phases should be regarded this way.

The first quarter phase has been called a 'crisis in action', indicating that at this point the individual questions for the first time his or her motives and the value of them. Like the adolescent, there may be a tendency to rebel here and to go completely against the natural flow of events. This would be a highly destructive possibility, resulting in this crisis of action. Will the individual go with the flow, or deliberately and destructively turn against it?

The last quarter phase has been called a 'crisis in consciousness' and it is at this point that the individual faces for the first time the possibility of death. From the fear that comes with the feeling of the black infinite depth of the unknown future, that heralds the forthcoming end of the cycle, a crisis occurs. Will the individual have the imagination and vision to see beyond the end of this cycle and into the next? Or will everything have been in vain, purposeless because no future design can be seen behind the grim eyes of death? Here the individual must choose whether or not to reorientate the aims of life towards the beginning of the next cycle. In such a case, death becomes a conscious crucifixion and resurrection, but, if vision is lacking, then the Ariadne thread of consciousness is lost and death becomes unconsciousness, an infinite sleep.

The birth chart will show the moon phase that was occurring at the time of birth and this symbolises the manner in which that person experiences the life-force as it flows through him or her. This archetypal cyclic pattern is traditionally interpreted by astrologers as reflecting the phase that an individual has reached in his or her own current cycle of evolution on the journey towards cosmic consciousness.

The phases of the moon have been used to represent the underlying pattern behind any cycle, no matter what it refers to and no matter how long the duration. For example, the *general* descriptions of the eight phases can be applied to the *particular* life cycle of each planet that will be described in Chapter 7. But first we will consider the cycle of life that applies to all of us, the life cycle of the individual.

CHAPTER 5
TWELVE STAGES OF LIFE

The astrological houses are usually described as representing areas of life, such as health, career, relationships, and so on. They can also be interpreted as representing 12 stages of development in the life cycle of the individual.

The orbital period of the planet Uranus is approximately 84 years. Traditional astrology regards this as representing a life span and divides it into 12 divisions of seven years each. There are several different astrological cycles that link with seven-year periods and perhaps coincidentally some psychologists recognise the existence of an approximate seven-year behaviour pattern or cycle of psychological growth related to the human psyche.

In order to describe the significance of each of the seven-year periods, I have associated them with the astrological houses of the birth chart, each of which represents an area of life, such as relationships, health, career, and so on. So in reading the following account of the growth process of the human psyche, the reader may also obtain some insight into the significance of the astrological houses, whose symbolism will be relevant to each particular period.

To make this clearer, imagine that we are following the planet Uranus on its (apparent) journey around the earth, a journey that takes 84 years to complete. We divide this period into 12 equal portions of seven years each and the distance of space covered during each seven-year period is called a 'house'. This is not exactly how the houses are defined when setting up and interpreting a birth chart, but the definition will suit our purposes here. It can now be seen how each of the houses, or seven-year periods, links closely with the symbolism of each sign of the zodiac, beginning with Aries (related to the first seven years and the 1st house) and progressing around the circle to finish with Pisces (related to the final period and the 12th house).

Age 0 to 7 and the 1st House

This period of life is one of forming and defining the shell that is to contain the personality. It is a highly extrovert period (Aries is a symbol of positive energy) for the young child has no consideration for itself and no sense of danger, but simply wishes to explore everything that it can see, feel, hear and touch. As far as the child is concerned, at first there is no clear definition as to what is child and what is surroundings, for a baby identifies itself closely with its sensory experiences. Slowly the ego forms and the formation of this ego and the personality structure that it contains depend almost entirely on the experience of immediate circumstances. Therefore, at this stage, the father and especially the mother play an important part in the personality formation. The astrological 1st house is traditionally associated with personality and influences with which the individual identifies itself. Hence the association with the first seven years of life, for during this period nothing else holds more importance.

At this time, the child is learning that he or she exists as an individual entity. Because the only way the child can assert any separateness and self-identity is through the experience of the environment itself, his or her personality becomes a reflection of that environment. He or she knows nothing of the world at large at this stage. The first seven years have an influence over the whole of the rest of the life span and it is only as one grows older that one can, in

94

retrospect, discover the prejudices or psychological complexes that stem from this period.

Age 7 to 14 and the 2nd house

This period is characterised by a realisation that the world is a big place and the individual but a tiny part of it. It is a period of introversion (Taurus is a negative energy) where the child becomes aware of the demands from elders to learn, develop and grow. The child must grow and keep up with friends of similar age and, not knowing whether or not this is possible, there are likely to be some feelings of insecurity.

At this stage the growing child is drawing nourishment from the surroundings in order to grow and develop and to do this needs a strong, well established contact with the sustaining nourishment that he or she draws upon. And here we see the link with the 2nd house, associated with Taurus. The 2nd house, or second area of life in this cycle of growth, is concerned with material security and the need for a definite relationship with the material world. Once this relationship and material security has been established, the child can then open itself to receive all the gifts of nourishment that the earth has to offer, whether on an intellectual, an emotional or a spiritual level of awareness.

The emphasis here is on growth. To the child this is an apparently slow and laborious process that seems never ending, but from an objective viewpoint it is only one necessary stage in the formation of a complete person and one which, from an adult, or retrospective viewpoint, takes place at a very rapid pace indeed. The growth experience during this period determines the stability of the future pattern – too much or too little stimulation can mean that the organism does not mature to its potential strength.

Age 14 to 21 and the 3rd house

The individual develops in this stage the ability and technique to open a responsive channel of communication with the surrounding environment and the people in it. This is the second extrovert period of exploration, but now on an intellectual rather than a sensory level. Associations are with the 3rd house and Gemini, a masculine, positive or extrovert energy. It is the period of adolescence where reactions as well as actions may now occur, such as rebellion against the rules and values of society. Not only does the person recognise that he or she is an individual, there is also a need to prove the uniqueness of this knowledge to others.

This period is often recognised as one of extreme concern for individuality and the adolescent may withdraw under a heightened awareness as being a person apart. Rebellion is the natural order and can be positively used to establish new modes of thought and activity, unrestricted by the moral conventions of a pre-established culture.

The third house is traditionally associated with the concrete mind and communication on a practical level, whereby the needs of the person can be stated and clearly defined. This statement may be in the manner of the rebellious adolescent but it should be listened to in all seriousness, for it heralds the breaking of new ground in the future from the point of view of a society or culture. Originality and the questioning of established modes of thought stimulates the evolution of life.

Age 21 to 28 and the 4th house

Now we come to the fourth seven-year period, when the direction of energy flow is introverted, a period where new-found freedom from parents and the home of childhood results in a need for the individual to establish his or her own home, a base which offers security, and somewhere to return to for protection from the harsh realities of the adult world. Not yet fully mature but no longer a child, the person here has perhaps to fend for himself or herself for the first time and it becomes imperative to look back, also for the first time, in order to establish the pattern so far and, in so doing, make firm the link or thread with the early home, with early childhood and, more importantly, with the cultural root or source of the individual.

The 4th house (linked with the introverted energy of Cancer) is traditionally associated with the home and childhood of the individual. The roots of the psyche have their source in the cultural heritage of society. The experience of this heritage is of a purely subjective nature, hence the emphasis is on introversion, on an inward search. On a more practical level, the individual here confronts the problems of adulthood and responsibility and also realises the infinite nature of possibilities in years to come. To cope with this pressure, the home becomes a place of refuge and protection against the pitiless elements of nature. The security that experience of this home or base has to offer is that of a definite link, or role within the pattern of things. No matter how small and insignificant the individual may seem in the light of an infinite universe, he or she still has a vital part to play in the drama of life and this knowledge imparts a sense of security.

Age 28 to 35 and the 5th house

This period marks the entrance of the individual upon the first stage of true adulthood. Basic skills have now been achieved, the channel is now ready and experience of the world and the self is sufficient to begin the process of self-expression in a creative and highly extroverted fashion. Now the individual experiences that he or she can really begin to live, conscious now of pattern and purpose.

This experience results in the need for self-expression, to create an expression for the reality of the self. And this is precisely what we find the definition of the 5th house affairs

97

to be; it is the area of life concerned with creativity and self-expression, from child-bearing to play-acting. This period of life (associated with Leo, a positive sign of creative Fire) is still ego-centred and fired by a desire to express uniqueness and individuality, but, being the first stage of maturity, there is some experience of the world at large on which to produce works of relevance for the masses. The artist, in satisfying the ego, may unwittingly satisfy that of his or her subjects, and hence we taste here also the first experience of a reality beyond the self, of the individuality and reality of other points of view.

Age 35 to 42 and the 6th house

This period may be one of deep, inner questioning, where the individual begins to examine all his or her motives and aims in life. This process is one of cleansing the conscious ego so that its future growth can take a wider, transcendent meaning. This marks, in astrological terms, the passage of the individual through the 6th house, associated with Virgo, an introverted Earth sign. In psychological terms it marks the period known as the mid-life crisis and indeed this has a strong link with the astrological map. The 6th house is the final area to be traversed before entering the second half of the circle around which we are moving through time.

The first half, through which we have so far been travelling, represents the subjective experience associated with the development of individuality. The second half (of life, or of the houses numbered 7 to 12) represents the objective role that the individual must play in terms of culture or the needs of society. Before the individual can adopt this role or purpose, he or she must undergo a process of self-questioning and purification, so that all actions taken as an individual are for the service of others.

This is the traditional meaning of the 6th house, known in fact as the 'house of service', and in traversing this period of life the individual is asked for the first time to recognise that the future is not for his or her benefit alone but is for humanity.

The inner questioning of motives and purposes may result in a personal revolution of awareness and an opportunity to encompass the possibility of new realities. Or the mid-life crisis may result in the hardening of the individual's beliefs and views, which may petrify and not permit future psychological growth. Many people develop inwardly no further than this, so that only a further crisis of greater proportions can have any effect in shifting the individual's viewpoint, allowing growth to continue.

The 6th house is the last in the first half of the cycle, and the crossing point between the 6th and 7th houses is a point of balance on the astrological map of the psyche.

Age 42 to 49 and the 7th house

The individual now knows the meaning of service, but this is of no use or value unless a relationship can be established between the self and the non-self, between the individual and the culture. On a material level, relationships during this period of life become particularly important for they reflect the manner in which the individual 'relates' in a wider context.

It is at this stage that the individual who has not achieved fulfilment through physical partnership may have to face all the problems that this may imply. This age period will then represent a 'last chance' to achieve a satisfaction of physical needs and security through the formation of a male/female relationship, or alternatively, it may represent the period of life when a consummated relationship brings forth the fruits of its growth.

The emphasis then is on relationship, not just in a physical sense but between ideas, between microcosm and macrocosm, between individual and society. A passage through the 7th house represents an entry into the social sphere of existence and an experience of the vital necessity

99

to form balanced relationships on all levels of being. To do this it is necessary to go out into the world, and hence this time of life is characterised by an extroverted pattern and is associated with Libra, a positive Air sign.

Age 49 to 56 and the 8th house

This period of life is the time when physical strength is waning, but as a complement to the waxing experience of inner strength and growth. During this time it is necessary to listen to the voice of this inner life as it begins to grow into a reality much more significant than that which is represented by the outer world of physical appearance.

This period is one of introversion, of seeking an inner source of strength and regeneration that lies beyond the individual ego. It is associated with the 8th house and with Scorpio, a negative Water sign.

It marks a necessity for integration of the self and the non-self, between the conscious personality and processes that lie within the unconscious. If this task is deliberately undertaken, then a new source of strength can be discovered which more than compensates for the dwindling of physical energy. In those who achieve this healthy, whole state of being can be seen perpetual youth shining through the light of their eyes, for through this process of individuation and integration they achieve an occult source of strength and may draw on its life-giving powers.

At this stage, instead of a dwindling of life the opposite should occur. This will take place if the individual is able to draw on a source that lies beyond the ego. This is the meaning in astrological symbolism of Scorpio and the 8th house. It is associated with energies that lie beyond the experience of the conscious ego and these can only be achieved through a process of death of the ego and rebirth of the self in a true integration with transpersonal forces.

Age 56 to 63 and the 9th house

The stage is now set for a passage through to the final period of life which we associate with maturity. The disease of our Western culture is to mark this period as an end of all that has been worked for. The individual is approaching retirement.

It should not be so, for this period of life marks the entrance into maturity and wisdom based on knowledge of experience. The total pattern should now become obvious, although it is not yet complete, and so now the individual should enter a period of life that is both creative and also fulfilling, not only for the individual but for society too.

It is important that we listen to and learn from the gifts of those who create from their experience of the total life pattern. This period can be the most creative, productive and valuable in terms of cultural benefit. It is associated astrologically with the 9th house. The area of life that this represents is to do with higher knowledge and philosophical wisdom. In other words, it is symbolic of teachings that stem from the individual who acts as a channel for wisdom that is of value on a wide-ranging scale. The individual at this 9th-house stage of life can be a wise teacher.

The 9th house is associated with Sagittarius, a positive Fire sign, and hence we have an indication that the period 56 to 63 years may be of extroversion, a final giving of inner gifts to the world of 'outer' experience.

Age 63 to 84 and the 10th, 11th and 12th houses

I have linked the final three periods of seven years together.

The 9th house period represented the final gift to society and, although this gift of creativity and self-expression originates from a higher realm, it is still of value to the material world. But now the gateway has been opened for the individual to commune with the Spirit and enter the final period of life which is a preparation for death.

This does not mean by any means that this period is fruitless – it is again only our mistaken Western culture and its misplaced materialistic ideals that tells us old age is a time for complete retirement. If the individual's imagination has avoided being stifled during his or her life, then this latter period of life can be the most important and most fruitful of all, for it is through the channel of the creative imagination that a relationship may be forged with that which lies beyond the ego self. It is to those who have recognised realities other than that assumed by the ego that this period of life brings forth its rewards. It is they who live beyond themselves, who have a vision of life and the infinite future who may move consciously through the final period of life.

Astrologically, the 10th house is linked with Capricorn and symbolises personal and social achievement; the 11th house is linked with Aquarius, and symbolises the ideals of freedom of spirit; and the final 12th house is linked with Pisces and symbolises self-sacrifice and death of the physical body.

This 12-fold model of the growth pattern reveals some interesting ideas. The pattern develops in seven-year periods that are alternately extrovert and introvert in their relationship with the zodiacal symbols, similar to a breathing process of inhalation and exhalation. Secondly, it emerges that instead of just one birth that an individual experiences during a single life-time, there can be three.

These three births are associated with the Fire houses, i.e. the 1st, 5th and 9th. The first is the physical birth, the second is the birth of true individuality and the third is the birth into spiritual awareness. This indicates that the archetypal life span can be divided into three main periods. From 0 to 28, the individual acts purely in response to cultural ideas and ideals, whether or not these actions are based on acceptance or rejection. From 28 to 56 the person acts as a true individual, if the rebirth process has been consciously acknowledged at about the age of 28.

At this time the first major life crisis may occur. What is born this time is not a physical child but an inner child of true individuality.

From the age of 56 to the end of life, the individual acts as a child of the spirit, if the third rebirth process has been acknowledged at about the age of 56. During this final period, a reintegration of individuality occurs, culminating in a return of the individual spirit to its source, as the physical body falls away at death.

The final observation that can be made from this model of the life cycle is that, in the same way that the signs of the zodiac and the astrological houses may form complementary pairs or polar opposites, so too may specific periods of life.

These polar opposites are:

Age 0–7 which complements age 42–49

Age 7–14 which complements age 49–56

Age 14–21 which complements age 56–63

Age 21–28 which complements age 63–70

Age 28–35 which complements age 70–77

Age 35–42 which complements age 77–84

In other words, the age 42 to 49, for example, will be a direct reflection of the age 0 to 7 – whatever was gained or lost, suppressed or expressed during the first seven years of life will need to be balanced by a complementary experience during the period of age 42 to 49, and so on. This implies that the model of the astrological houses can be an aid to probing the root cause or the initial imbalance of a current life situation by exploring the complementary period of life. This also indicates that the age 0 to 42 is one of sowing, while the period thereafter is one of reaping the products of whatever were sown during the first period of life, a statement which takes on greater significance when explored in terms of the seven-year divisions that constitute the cycle of life.

It is also possible to see now how this cycle of life, as related to the individual, can be superimposed on the archetypal lunation cycle, which iterates and amplifies the different phases and crisis points within the cycle.

Having considered the nature of cyclic processes as they apply to the individual, we can now turn to examine the zodiac and see how its story can add to our knowledge of the life cycle.

CHAPTER 6
THE ZODIAC – FROM BIRTH TO DEATH

Not only are there the daily patterns of life and those longer ones recognised with maturing years, but there is also a greater, cosmic cycle of life and death that the zodiac describes. It does so in such a way that the greater unfolding of the universe can be part of the inner growth and development of the individual. The zodiac can reveal the purpose of life and its patterns.

The zodiac contains in its symbolism perhaps the richest story of unfoldment known to us. Its pattern begins with the simple, single, whole form of the circle from Aries to Pisces containing within it mathematical intricacies of great beauty and significance formed by the many interweaving relationships of the 12 zodiacal archetypes.

Written in the zodiac is the history of human consciousness, its purpose, its goal. The stars reflect back to us the way we see ourselves and are a mirror, rather like the looking-glass of Alice, through which we must pass in order to discover the substance of their reflection. Stepping through the looking-glass means entering a world of the imagination where the only rule is that there are no physical laws to govern, limit or control our progress. Each of us is on a unique journey, a journey through life, and, if we can somehow endure its perils until the end, it will lead us to what we have been searching for.

To be on a journey, searching for something that may not exist, along a special path that could be one of an infinite number of possibilities, and to do this perhaps without even knowing it – in terms of rational thought, this makes no sense. When trying to fathom the most difficult questions about life, however, we are dealing with a subject that is greater than the rational mind can cope with, that steps beyond its limits. The answers to questions such as 'Who am I?' 'What is my purpose?' 'Where am I going?' lie beyond the realms of the rational mind.

The study of the relationship between the stars, the planets and humankind is the study of our journey through life and the path that may be followed in achieving an awareness of harmony between polar opposites, inner and outer, feminine and masculine, fate and free will, so that an awareness of the complete picture can be achieved that includes both sides of the story.

The signs of the zodiac are displayed in such a way that there is a story of birth, growth, death and rebirth told by its symbols. This cycle of life can be interpreted on any scale. It can represent a day, a year or the lifetime of an individual, as the planets, the sun and the moon progress each on their own journey through the stars. Or it can be seen as the cycle of world history and the eras through which the world passes.

Astrology is a study of cycles that lead from beginnings to ends to new beginnings, and the knowledge of these cycles provided for us by astrologers through the ages can be used to study the development of a single person or of humanity as a whole, through the study of our relationship with the life of the stars. As above, so below – the microcosm is a reflection of the macrocosm, for we are inextricably linked with it, caught up in the web of life and must go with its flow or break the delicate infrastructure of that finely woven web.

There is a cycle of growth on earth that is easily apparent and observable to us and this is the progression of the four seasons through each year. It was the cycle of the seasons that people first observed when learning how to adapt their behaviour in order to flow with the natural course of life – so that they weren't planting seed when they should have been harvesting grain in the ripening heat of the summer sunshine.

In modern life, many of us have lost touch with the natural rhythms of nature, but they are there all the same and even live and move within each of us as we move from the springtime of childhood to the winter of old age. So, even though we do not think we live at the beck and call of the elements, the cycle of nature is of vast importance to our inner life and growth. The seasons of the sun are an inner as well as an outer process and experience.

There were civilisations that knew this and therefore tried to synchronise their lives with the forces of nature through the rites and ceremonies devised by the priests or Druids who formed the link between the forces of heaven and the working man and woman on earth. When the link was forged, the gods worked with them and their harvest was a success. Now, on an individual, a national and a planetary level, it is time for us to stop trying to conquer nature. We should co-operate with her and move gently through the seasons of life, travel through the never-ending cycles of time, experience the perpetual return to the place from which we started until, to quote T.S. Eliot, we know the place for the first time.

Each season is an initiation. When the initiations are complete, then our body, mind and spirit experience unity, wholeness, and we are healed on both the physical and ethereal planes. I would like to take you on a journey around the cycle of the seasons so that perhaps the healing forces within it can be evoked.

Winter

The starting time is the period before the new birth when winter, old age and reflection on the past reign supreme. The winter period begins in this calendar mid-way through Scorpio, a time marked by festivals, by Hallowe'en and All

Saints. It is the time when, to the ancient Celts and the priestly order of Druids, the Earth Mother turns from the Great Provider to the Great Devourer and assumes her form as the Old Hag, the winter goddess. The forces that play upon the earth are drawn into her and she needs to protect and nurture the seed that lies dormant within her womb.

The winter period is born in Scorpio, a Water sign, and winter is ruled by this element whose colour is blue and whose experience or initiation is the control of the emotions so that we can find peace. The symbol for Scorpio, the scorpion, becomes transmuted to the eagle when the insight of Scorpio can be lifted to fly at such a height that it sees all, like the eagle flying high above the earth. But the vision of Scorpio can be lifted even higher, so that what the eagle sees is its purpose and then the eagle becomes transformed into the dove, the bringer of peace. When we have achieved the dove, then the troubled waters of the emotions are stilled and when that ocean becomes calm it is possible to see the life that exists below its surface. The sea is a symbol for the unconscious mind, so now its hidden depths stand revealed when Scorpio achieves the dove and the peace that it brings. Only then can the truth be penetrated.

Perhaps now we dive into the sea of the unconscious, only to find that we are lost, even drowning perhaps. We manage to make our way to the surface once more and breathe the air. But the experience never leaves us, we are reborn, regenerated and ready to move on while Gabriel, the archangel of winter, watches over us.

We move on next into Sagittarius. Perhaps during the winter there is time to reflect upon the whole pattern, to try to encompass the earth and the heavens in one fell swoop of vision. This is what Sagittarius seeks to do, to explore and know all that the earth has to offer while aiming high at a target that is way beyond the sight of mortals. Sagittarius is the fiery philosopher who works with the abstract mind, trying to perfect thought, the tool that has been given to the human race to do with as we choose. Perhaps in the same way that birds fly, the human thinks. But, as T.H. White has pointed out, the birds seem to have perfected flight, while we lag far behind. Be that as it may, we must aim the arrow high if we are to hope to achieve perfection.

It is worth noting here that the polar opposite of Sagittarius is Gemini. This pair illustrates the polar activity at work throughout the whole cycle of the zodiac; its symbols show that there are always two sides to a story, and these are inextricably linked. The other side of Sagittarius then is Gemini, ruler of the concrete mind, of communication on an immediate level. While Sagittarius tries to encompass the whole in one go, Gemini tries to achieve the same end by sampling all the constituent parts, like a butterfly moving haphazardly through a field of flowers trying to settle on all of them. Here we have two aspects of the same thing, in this case of the mind. Sagittarius represents the abstract mind, the philosopher; Gemini represents the concrete mind, the divider.

The winter is passing by and suddenly a change catches our attention and we enter the time of Capricorn, marked by the festivals of the winter solstice and Christmas. We are at the heart of winter, although our modern calendar would show it as only just beginning. We are at winter's depth, before the gradual turn towards the future and the germination of a new seed in the springtime.

In esoteric astrology, Capricorn is known as one of the 'Great Gates' and through it a person may pass from the earth plane to those of the Universal Spirit where he or she can once more commune with God. Through its polar opposite, Cancer, another of the Great Gates, a person is said to move in the opposite direction, to enter upon the Wheel of Life, to descend to physical earth and assume the form and limitations of a man or woman who must learn that he or she is going to die. Only through the realisation of earthly limits and acceptance of the laws that govern life will that inevitable death be raised to the heights of the eternal life and he or she can move through the Great Spiritual Gate of Capricorn.

Traditionally, Capricorn is ruled by the grim figure of Saturn, and is a symbol linked with the formation of structure. Once Sagittarius has formed an abstract philosophy, it must be put to use in Capricorn in forming a workable, political system within which people can live and work. It seems strange at first glance that Capricorn should be designated Gateway to the Stars, but hidden here is a major lesson of life, an initiation. Before we can go beyond a structure, we must learn to accept it, to know its, or our, limits. Accept your place on earth, do your best within it and know that you cannot defy the laws of nature. But realise also that, even though these appear to be limitations, there is something beyond. Even though caught up in a winter that seems so barren and lifeless, lying dormant is a seed, waiting until the time is right to germinate, to embark upon a new cycle and enter into springtime, shedding the protection of winter.

Spring

The next initiation in the cycle of life is the spring. This period begins half-way through Aquarius, a time marked by Candlemas at the beginning of February and which sees the beginning of new life all around us. The first flowers of the year begin to penetrate above ground level and spring is in the air. For Aquarius is an Air element whose colour is yellow and which rules the springtime of life, over which the archangel Raphael, the Healer, assumes his place. The experience, the initiation of Air, is in learning the lesson of brother and sisterhood.

This is particularly significant today as the Age of Aquarius approaches and we need to discover what its lessons are to be; brother and sisterhood is living with not only our fellow people but with all forms of life, with the planet as a whole. The Age of Wars is drawing to a close. After the battle to assert ourselves is over and the springtime of human life takes form, perhaps we will begin to see the world through freshly opened eyes. Aquarius is the sign of humanity, of an awareness of group living, and we can see the experiments of this going on now, of global rather than nationalistic awareness.

Here again, the polar opposite of Aquarius, which is Leo, must not be forgotten. Leo represents the individual, and the creativity and value of each individual. This means that although the emphasis of Aquarius is on the group, on world-wide citizenship, we must respect the balancing factor and the rights of the individual. Human rights are of prime importance if brotherhood is to be achieved and this will be a long process. The winter is slowly dying and, when it is dead, the children of spring, of the New Age, will understand what is needed.

Spring and the element of Air are also an initiation into understanding. The ageless wisdom remains true through all time, even though our interpretation of its meaning must change and evolve. An appropriate example is that of astrology, a subject whose symbols were at risk of losing their life and energy as it became a subject no longer relevant to the modern view of reality. Viewpoints on all subjects have become too one-sided; the polar opposites have been tearing one another apart instead of balancing in harmony. Science needs the feeling and depth of art; humanity must nurture the individual; Aquarius and Leo must work together.

After Aquarius, we enter Pisces, the most watery of the Water signs, and again we are confronted with the possibility of losing ourselves in the waters of the unconscious, of letting go of worldly cares and sacrificing ourselves to the cause of humanity established by Aquarius. But if we are to remain on our path, Pisces must be used in a different way.

The symbolism of Pisces is associated with the collective unconscious, a sea that is available to us all and upon which we may draw, through the conscious use of the imagination and through our dreams. From this realm can be channelled insight and inspiration – the mystical experience of the nature of reality that encompasses both the conscious and the unconscious self.

Now the spring enters its peak at the equinox as we move into the time of Aries, the sign of the zodiac that bubbles with life, that says no more with cares, death, philosophising, structures, grey skies or sadness. Aries just wants to get on with living and knows how actions speak louder than words. The spring is here, so let's get on with springtime, with growing, exploring, shouting and laughing with the joys of new life and the birth of a New Age. Through the adolescent, pure strength of Arien energy, the spring finds an impetus to move beyond the pains of early growth, towards maturity and the summer months that will reveal the harvest produced by the labours of the people and those of nature. When these two work together, they achieve maturity and a ripening of both the human soul and the fruits of the earth – but we have not quite reached this stage of autumnal harvest, as first we must move through the time of ripening of the fruit by summer sunshine.

Summer

The next initiation we come to in the cycle of life that the seasons of the year depict in poetic detail is that of summer. The summer months can be likened to the period in life that corresponds to newly achieved manhood or womanhood, the period between adolescence and the autumn months of maturity.

During the summer, the earth demonstrates in full glory all that she is capable of producing. Beginning half-way through Taurus, with Ascension Day and the May Day festivals, and watched over by the archangel Uriel, the summer is a time of awareness of the Earth element and all that it can bring forth into being, all that the earth can provide for us to live, if we are prepared to work and replenish its needs in return. The laws of karma, of action and reaction, apply in our relationship with the planet on which we live, as well as in our personal relationships. The summer is ruled by the Earth element, whose colour is green. It is the time when the Earth Goddess assumes the form of the Earth Maiden whose childhood must be sacrificed to the gods in order to achieve womanhood, and the turning of flower into fruit for the autumn picking. The earth gives forth in plenty and to ensure a rich harvest the laws of karma must be satisfied by a sacrifice: 'Oh Goddess, we offer thee this sacrifice. Give to us good seasons, crops and health.'

The initiation found through the element of Earth is an initiation into matter as an expression of the spirit. The 'matter' of the physical body includes the subtle bodies and may be seen as a monitor of their condition, or well-being. We are concerned here with helping the spirit gain mastery over physical matter and the lesson taught is a practical one of service. Note the paradox, the balancing polarity – to gain mastery, service must be given.

Taurus traditionally is the sign of the Bull who must plough the earth and serve his master. We are that Bull and must serve our master, must work hard in order to bring forth the fruits of the earth. After Aries enthusiasm must come the hard work. Venus is the planet that rules Taurus, a strange combination at first sight, for the brute strength of the Bull to be linked closely with the beauty of Venus. But Venus has many faces, and in Taurus she is the young Earth Maiden who will turn the labours of the Bull into the beauty of that which grows and flowers.

In experiencing the Earth initiation through the summer months of life, we move next through Gemini, the sign of the Twins, who show us that everything which comes into being in the physical world is dual in nature, has a twin that walks with it wherever it may go. But even duality has its twin – non-duality, unity, the place from which the Twins sprang and to which they must return by the laws of nature.

Taurus builds and Gemini communicates, the messages being taken to and fro by Mercury, ruler of Gemini and winged messenger of the gods.

The summer period reaches its peak at the midsummer solstice as we now enter Cancer to the accompaniment of much Dionysian feasting and celebration. Cancer is ruled by the moon, the celestial body that receives and reflects the rays of the sun – symbol of the higher self – to earth, or the physical plane. We have been following the course of the yearly cycle of the sun through the seasons, but the moon has a rhythm of her own, a cyclic pattern that is also linked with the sun's movement but which completes a full cycle each lunar month.

If we were to relate the cycle of the season to the lunation cycle, we would have new moon to first quarter phase as springtime, first quarter to full moon as the summer, full moon to last quarter as the autumn and last quarter to new moon as wintertime.

The cycles of the moon and sun are close to our lives and we should heed them closely if we wish to tune in and link with forces that are beyond the normal field of consciousness.

But now we are to enter upon the final phase of our journey through the seasons. We could have begun at any point on the circle, but wherever it had begun it would inevitably have returned to that point. The way back is through the autumn as the nights begin to close in once more and life's harvest reflects the gold of the sun.

Autumn

From Cancer, the sign of the moon, our attention moves next to Leo, the sign of the sun. We enter the autumn time of maturity beginning at the Lammas Harvest Festivals of early August, mid-way through Leo. It is no chance occurrence that the queen of the zodiac, the moon, and its king, the sun, should sit side by side and go hand in hand, the former Water, the latter Fire. And it is Fire whose colour is red which is the element associated with the autumn period.

114

Autumn, a period of fermentation and inner warmth, is watched over by the archangel Michael, Herald of Transformation and Bearer of the Light.

Initiation by Fire is to understand the primal essence of the spirit which is love. Fire teaches the lesson of love; wisdom must have been learnt already, so that the fire of love is not a destructive, all-consuming agent, but can be used wisely. Love is the magic fire that was stolen by Prometheus from the altar of the gods, it is the light of the sun, it is music, harmony, energy and above all it is illumination.

The autumn fire begins with the golden corn and ends with a fiery carpet of leaves that fall to earth to await the devouring winter goddess who must inevitably return in the guise of the Old Hag, of death. But first the harvest – a wedding followed by the fruits of that wedding between heaven and earth. The creative principle of manhood is seen at work and being made manifest. The Maiden matures and becomes the Earth Mother and now the linking thread becomes apparent which weaves its way through all the seasons from Old Hag to Child, then Maiden and now to the Earth Mother who is on the verge of growing old again.

Our culture during the last two stages, during the Ages of Aries and Pisces, has lost touch with this female principle, with the Earth Goddess, because of the over-dominance of the sun, of the male principle, which has used rational thought and even brute strength to enforce its will. The earth has been neglected and raped, and the signs of this are everywhere. We are perhaps beginning to take note through necessity. The domineering father is learning once more that he needs the mother in order to become whole and healthy. Intuition and feelings must take their place alongside the intellect and dominance by strength, otherwise the earth itself will rebel and become barren.

We must ensure, however, that the pendulum does not swing too far in the other direction. The moon and the sun, the female and the male, should be together.

Time passes now from Leo into Virgo, sign of the Virgin

who is ripe for the picking, the fruit that must be harvested. Traditionally, Virgo is the sign of service. Although in this sign we meet again Mercury as the ruling planet, esoteric astrologers have placed Vulcan as the ruler of this sign, the mighty Vulcan who provided the gods with armour and weapons of perfection that were created through love of the materials with which he worked. Mythology tells us how Vulcan suffered humiliation in learning what his place in life was to be, but, once he had found it, his enormous strength was used to produce metalwork of the finest precision. Through the love of service, perfection was achieved.

Next we move at the autumn equinox into Libra, the most peaceful of the zodiacal signs, and we again encounter Venus as the ruler. This time, Venus is in her more familiar form as the embodiment of aesthetic appreciation, of relationship and harmony and therefore of balance. The scales of Libra weigh all that has gone before and, if they are in balance, peace reigns. The perfection of Virgo is placed in the scales of Libra and is found to be balanced by the love of the goddess Venus. The last lesson has been learnt. The purification of the Fire initiation is complete. But life must go on, for this is a cycle which will continue. It is fitting that the end point and the new beginning as we leave Libra should be Scorpio again, for although it is the barren winter that approaches, Scorpio is the sign of regeneration, of the phoenix that will arise once more. Perhaps the message of the seasons is that only through death can life be found that is everlasting.

This cycle of the seasons shows how astrology relates the movement of the sun to man's own life, how the outer life of the universe is a reflection of the inner experience of the individual, the world of the spirit that may be called the inner life of matter. The planets and stars set a greater pattern and allow its healing energy to work through us.

Healing through the symbols of this wisdom depends first of all on an acknowledgement that we are part of the greater whole, yet also possessing within us the possibility

116

of achieving our own unique capabilities, of becoming a whole person. Secondly, there must be a desire to attune to the larger pattern so that we can work with it, and through this ritual know that life has meaning. Even though that meaning cannot be defined simply by a rational process, it is a meaning that must be discovered through each of the four elements, through thought, feeling, sensation and intuition – the functions of personality that correspond to Air, Water, Earth and Fire.

The cycle of the zodiac forms a background against which the planets, the sun and moon, appear to circle the earth and each of these can reveal the patterns of life that not only re-occur on a day-to-day, or yearly basis but which bring the major lessons of life. These lessons, or initiations, described by the planets, will be the subject of the next chapter.

CHAPTER 7

PLANETS OF THE MIND

Each planetary symbol is associated with particular human attributes or qualities. For example, Venus rules sexual pleasures and bestows aesthetic appreciation. The planets of inner space also have their own cycles of unfoldment, affecting the changing circumstances of human life. Each can be considered in terms of the lessons and experiences they bring.

This chapter describes the nature of the planetary beings through the allegory of a story, a journey through the planets. The idea of the planets as independent 'personalities' within the unconscious was introduced in the section on meditation and guided imagery in Chapter 2. To expand on these personalities further, as each is encountered there is an accompanying description giving the basic interpretation of the function, personality, background mythology, sexual characteristics and life cycles of each planet.[1]

As an archetypal symbol, an eclipse marks the time before a new dawn, the darkness that enfolds a seed of cosmic light, the rediscovery of the process of enlightenment. After the eclipse, the primordial chaos or *nigredo* of the alchemist, come the colours, each leading towards a final integration as the sun or 'gold' stage is reached. Each planet may be

---

1. A particularly interesting exercise is to use a diary to record and investigate any personal cycles that can be identified with those of particular planets. Remember that the development of each *particular* cycle follows the *general* pattern of phases described in Chapter 4. The astrological interpretation of these planetary cycles is also given in detail in such books as Betty Lundsted's *Planetary Cycles* and Alexander Ruperti's *Cycles of Becoming*.

experienced as a lamp illuminating the road that leads to the sun, the Self, the One Light. Each planetary symbol in our solar system can be seen to act as a signpost along the way from point to point on our journey to the Self.

In looking towards the planets for guidance, we are also delving deep inside ourselves, into the unconscious, where the laws of the exoteric universe no longer apply, but where a new type of law is discovered. This might be called 'cosmic law', and is a law of synchronicity that links the inner universe of the individual with objective reality. Again, each planet can indicate to us the nature of a particular law at work governing the path of transformation and enlightenment. The mystic studies cosmic law. The scientist studies the laws of nature. Each sees the world from a different point of view and the point where they meet, the point of transcendence, is in the symbol. One might say that the scientist regards gravity as a pull towards the centre of the earth, whereas the mystic regards gravity as a push from the rest of the universe.

This then concludes the theory. Let me now take you, stage by stage, along the journey towards our destination which is Gold.

I shall describe this journey using an alchemical allegory as the means for relating the process of unfoldment. This allegory is linked with significant power points around the British Isles. Along the way we shall meet the planetary beings who represent cosmic laws and how we can become aware of their power through an alchemical transformation of the mind. These forces of transformation are there waiting for us to acknowledge their presence, waiting to act as guides along the way. Who will dare to venture with me along the path to meet with these mythical beings whose power is cosmic?

THE MOON

Function

The main purpose of the moon is to give form and substance to the life force. The sun provides the initial impulse, but it is the moon that makes this impulse fertile and gives it material expression. The moon is a reflective, feminine archetype whose function is to respond, to nurture and to give form. Astrologically often associated with the mother, the moon also symbolises the past, memories and childhood.

Personality

Positive—The moon is sensitive to change and adapts easily to changes in the moods of others. She is protective, emotionally deep and changeable. Closely in touch with her inner world of dreams and the unconscious she is also highly sensitive to the realities of the outer world. She is impressionable, sympathetic, receptive, modest and kind.

Negative—Emotional sensitivity can become moodiness, with a tendency to emotional outbursts. The moon may be unstable and unreliable, prone to fantasies. Her touchiness may result from a weak will, indecisiveness and her prejudices. The moon is not dogmatic, but conversely she may be easily influenced and unpredictable.

Mythology

The moon was worshipped, usually as the Great Mother, or Mother Earth, and was represented by: Arterius, Astarte, Demeter, Hera, Hecate, Selene (Greek); Isis (Egyptian); Diana, Ceres, Juno (Roman); Freyr (Nordic); Ishtar (Sumero-Akkadian); Metztli (Aztec); Parvati, Soma (Hindu).

Sexual characteristics

It is the mysterious and sensitive nature of the moon that makes her attractive to the male sex. Also her characteristics as the protective mother may enhance this. She represents one masculine ideal, being soft, yielding, responsive, nurturing, sympathetic and open to the penetrating seed of the male principle.

Life cycle and crisis points

Cycle: 28 days.

Crisis points—In terms of long-lasting effects, this must be considered a minor cycle. It is most useful to consider the moon phases (the lunation cycle of 29½ days), whose points of tension are the full and new moons in particular. The full moon is a notorious time for increase in violent crimes, a response to stress and uncontrollable impulses.

MOON STATION

It is dark. The full moon is hidden behind a cloud, giving it a silvery-white edge. I can hardly see my way as I walk slowly along the avenue towards dim white figures. On either side I am guided past dark, looming shapes, the cold standing stones of Callanish that lead towards the circle. I stop and watch the strange movements of 12 figures within the circle, movements that express forces so powerful that my mind, for its own safety, must suppress any recognition of them. I know these movements and their meaning, but my mind tells me they are a mystery.

The figures part, the full face of the moon appears low on the horizon and I see a woman now bathed in moonlight whose beauty compels me to move forward and stand before her. She wears a silver gown and raises her hand in greeting.

'I am the Moon. I am the Goddess of Moon and Magic, I

am Isis, Chandra Devi, Nana, Ceres, Diana and Mother of Christ. My Law is the Law of Rhythm which you, the traveller who comes to bathe in my light, must understand. The Law of Rhythm is of perpetual cycles: of night following day, of day following night, of the dance of life and death. When you work with my Law you will see where you are going, for you will know where you have come from and will perceive the harmony and beauty of the universe as it ebbs and flows to the constant rhythms of creation. You must know and accept your place and the part that you play in the sea of life whose tides are compelled by my Law. Align yourself with your Self and you need then make no effort, for the tide will take you to your destination. You need do nothing except find the direction of the flow and go with it, and then you will achieve everything.

'To perceive the Law of Rhythm is the first step. To go further, you must look with eyes that see beyond the cycles of the rhythm, see through our sacred ritual that brings the perpetual return of the seasons and the renewal of life. You are caught on the Wheel of Life. Know that this Wheel has a still centre. This is your aim. Turn towards the centre.

'Follow my Ray, the Silver Ray, for this Ray will illumine your path with a light that leads both from and to the Gold of the Sun.'

And thus saying, the high priestess and her druids vanished from sight. I moved to where she stood and found growing there a circle of mushrooms and at their centre lay a single pearl, a stone of the moon. All around the light was flowing, a river of silver-grey, white, pale greens and blues, shimmering and swirling, and from out of this river of light there arose the vision of a white rose and I understood all that she had said.

We have begun the journey and found a direction at the Moon Station. It is to lead us away from what we are, to what we are to become. We have therefore to re-orient ourselves. We have to reach the dark side of the moon, with eyes riveted to the Star.

MERCURY

Function

Mercury is a symbol for the processes of thought and the intellect, and of communication of ideas. It represents the concrete mind. The influence of Mercury can be seen at work in the sciences where quantities of data are categorised and analysed, so that the laws governing order in nature can be discovered and communicated. This is the traditional astrological interpretation, but, as an energy of the psyche, Mercury is more than this. Jung called this archetype the 'Trickster' and as such Mercury represents uncertainty – in anything to do with the rational mind there is always an element of doubt. Although these 'trickster' qualities of Mercury are difficult to pin down, the planet has also been endowed with the power to heal.

Personality

Positive—Mercury has great analytical ability, and is versatile and perceptive with a natural inquisitiveness. This is also demonstrated through Mercury's ability as a communicator of great eloquence and wit. A youthful lover of jokes and pranks, Mercury is lively and mentally energetic.

Negative—Boundless mental and nervous energy can result in a restless and unreliable disposition, prone to be critical and meddlesome. Mercury also has a side which has cunning, and this, coupled with great mental agility, can lead to the art of deception.

Mythology

Mercury in mythology was often associated with commerce, science and education, and was represented by: Hermes (Greek); Mercury (Roman); Nebo (Babylonian); Odin (Nordic); Wotan (Germanic).

123

Sexual characteristics

Mercury exhibits qualities of both male and female, but is usually depicted as male. He is young, healthy, lively and bright, offering great physical attraction to the opposite sex in the same aesthetic sense as the sun. Mercury's flighty, fickle behaviour can be attractive from a distance but, once ensnared by him, he will leave without a moment's notice, though not before giving a dazzling display of flattery.

Life cycle and crisis points

Cycle: approximately 365 days.

Crises—The short cycle of Mercury means that crisis points are insignificant.

MERCURY STATION

And now the light changed and it was as if the whole world was bathed in a metallic blue, a light of electrifying energy that hummed with the force of life. Then I perceived that I was the centre of a field of radiating lines of violet that shot out from me, as if I were the hub of a wheel and they the spokes, although I could perceive no rim.

I could still feel the ground below my feet, but could see nothing, except the radiating streams of violet in their field of metallic blue. Then I heard the voice that seemed to come from within, but it was so elusive that it may have come from beyond my field of vision. Were my ears playing tricks on me? All I could do was listen.

'I am Mercury. I am the Magician and the luck-bringing messenger of the immortals. I am the hottest, nearest and quickest at 108,000 miles per hour. I am the Monkey God, the Trickster who stole Apollo's sheep, the girdle of Venus, the tongs of Vulcan and the trident of Neptune. I am the fleet-footed messenger of the gods through whom you may communicate with the depths of your being. For see here, I hold a mirror and whosoever shall look into this mirror shall learn that he has another half that spells infinity. But you shall not simply look. Come, you may step into the mirror so that you will learn the workings of my Law, the Law of Duality, which says that within nothing can be perceived the makings of the universe, and yet (here's the trick) our universe is a mere nothing. Tread lightly, my friend, for I fly close to the sun and there is danger from that devouring presence at whose centre is a void, black nothingness.

'If you will acknowledge my presence, I will reveal to you the nature of reality on your plane of being. Know that if you are striving for all that is good, then you must acknowledge the force of evil. It is not enough simply to do good, for you must meet both sides of yourself, meet also the reality of evil, of your own evil, a part of you that cannot be denied. The cutting blade of Mercury reveals good and evil and the light which lies like a seed within darkness, a seed that will germinate when, later on your journey, you pass through the darkness of Saturn. But for now, all I can say to you is pass into the mirror and walk with the ghostly images that lie therein so that you might learn the nature of their reality.

'It is not enough for you to look into the mirror, for it, like your intellect, will simply show you an image of yourself – a likeness not a reality. Pass into the mirror of Mercury, travel along my Ray, the Mirror Ray, and you will discover the reality that lies within illusion.'

And thus the voice of Mercury seemed to show me how his mirror reflected the light of the Star to which I must go, and these reflections became the earth ley lines, the violet lines which I could see now stretched far and wide, super-imposed on the surrounding countryside.

At this stage of the journey, the One becomes Two through the cutting blade of Mercury. Polar opposites and duality enter awareness and at this station I was lost, for I could no longer see the earth. But the words of Mercury helped me to rediscover myself and enter upon the Path of

125

Return. Echoes of these words filled my mind: 'To see utter darkness and desperate anguish and yet respond in understanding and in love while holding fast to the Way is to pass beyond the Mercury Station.'

As I continued on my journey, a gentle scent of lavender filled the air.

VENUS

Function

The purpose of Venus is to bring harmony and form relationships. This urge can be between people or between a person and any object of his or her desire. Venus rules erotic love and feelings in the realm of human relationships. The principle is also a bestower of aesthetic appreciation and a sense of value, but not in a material sense.

Personality

Positive—Venus is co-operative, artistic, compassionate and amorous. She will offer kindness and sympathy and has an empathy for all aesthetic values and appeal. She is gentle and refined in all her affairs, displaying artistry both in the way she conducts her relationships and in her refined appearance.

Negative—Amorousness can turn to self-indulgence and immorality. She can be vain and lustful, with no thought for the objects of her self-indulgence.

Mythology

Venus, as the goddess of love and beauty, was represented by Aphrodite (Greek); Istar (Sumero-Akkadian); Venus (Roman); Freyja (Nordic); Frigg (British).

Sexual characteristics

Venus is the epitomy of feminine beauty, but whereas the moon is motherly and mature, Venus is young, gregarious, flirtatious and extremely amorous. She loves to be worshipped for her beauty and will allow the indulgence of her admirers.

Life cycle and crisis points

Cycle: 225 days.

Crises—Venus and Mercury align closely with the sun. The short cycle means that crisis points are short lived.

VENUS STATION

Daybreak and a prayer for Lucifer, Herald of the Light. I knelt before an altar at a point of power in the heart of England – Whitley Church, where paintings of great beauty adorn the walls and ceilings, a place for contemplation and for thanksgiving to the patroness of the arts, to Venus, the Morning Star. With this in mind, I was transported to a wondrous planet, where a day is longer than a year, where clouds were bending the sun's light, creating a strange optical illusion. I could see the sun rising over the horizon from my vantage point and yet behind me, simultaneously, it was setting too. My attention was then distracted by the soft voice of a young woman whose beauty rivalled that of the moon, who wore precious stones of beryl, jade and lapis lazuli, and bands of copper around her neck and arms. Strangely, she seemed to be expecting me, and was ready to act as my guide and reveal the meaning of her beauty.

'Understand now my nature. Mercury the electric force, Venus the magnetic – together they constitute the electromagnetic field that draws chaotic energy into patterns. I am the line of force which may be made manifest by the patterns of matter that correspond to it. Mine is the Law of Correspondence. As above, so below. I give to you the knowledge of beauty, for in each event on your earth plane may be seen the story of a cosmic event, while in each planet or star may be found a correspondence with life on earth. In the falling of an autumn leaf there is a cosmic truth. In an eclipse of the sun lies the dawning of a new age.

'It is in me that the true process begins, for I can refine the nature of your understanding. Through me can the essence be extracted. Watch my alchemy as a ray of sunlight falls on the earth from which a seed grows to a flower and sap becomes nectar, which the bee extracts and converts to honey. I am the Queen of the Bees and it was from me that the bees issued forth and came to your earth.

'Your task, through my Ray, the Magnet Ray, is to draw these celestial bees to you, so that they may extract your spiritual nectar and transform it into honey. This is the alchemy and the transmutation that takes place within my Hive of Flames.'

And with these words I was transported once more to my prayer at the altar. Through the window I could see that the passage of time had been such that the Morning Star was now twinkling in a dusky sky and had been transformed into Hesperus, the Evening Star.

I understood now the meaning of value, for value was a line of force, the Magnet Ray of Venus, which may be clothed with artistic form. Through this realisation, personal values take on a new significance and purpose – it is no longer I who lives; God lives in me. Now the path is no longer centred on the earth, or geocentric, it is centred on the sun, has a heliocentric point of view. I am no longer the centre of myself, but there is another centre of consciousness, the heliocentric self.

I stepped from the Venus Station out of the church, into a grove of ash and cyprus trees. Through the branches of the trees the light filtered in pastel shades of blue, green and yellow.

MARS

Function

Mars is the archetype of power and motivation and manifests most obviously in leaders of men. This does not mean that the Mars archetype is weak in women, but our culture encourages it in the male sex and it often lies dormant in the female. The will to succeed, whether in a career, in a physical activity or in a relationship, is motivated by Mars.

Personality

Positive—Mars is active, courageous and pioneering. He will assert himself through great ambitions and will thrive on competition. He has a persuasive manner and an appealing spontaneity.

Negative—Power and motivation can result in an aggressive, coarse, domineering character, and ambition may manifest as militance if he is thwarted. Mars may be reckless and wilful, with no care for the consequences of his impatient actions.

Mythology

Mars, as the god of war, was represented by: Ares (Greek); Mars (Roman); Indra (Hindu); Odin (Nordic); Attis-Adonis (Asia-Minor).

Sexual characteristics

Mars is the masculine ideal of masculinity, a man's man, with an athletic body and mind. He is domineering in sexual relationships and his insensitivity and dogmatic rule may or may not prove attractive, according to taste.

Life cycle and crisis points

Cycle: 2–2½ years.

Crises—The pattern of the Mars cycle can be used to develop skills, enhance career, or improve relationships. The fairly short cycle of approximately two and a half years means that repeating patterns can be easily observed and used for personal benefit.

MARS STATION

I next found myself at the foot of a hill in Glastonbury. I climbed up it to a tower that had been built on its summit. All around were flat planes, a mandala of the world. An unearthly wind blew so strongly that I had to seek shelter against the leeward wall of the tower. I was overtaken by a profound weariness, a tiredness not only of the body but of the soul too, and I felt the effects of everything that had gone before and the shattering this had caused of all that I thought I was. I felt done for and desperately in need of help. I remembered that near the tor on which I stood was a well, known as the Chalice Hill Well, and I knew that for some reason I must go there.

I stood before this well and looked at the magic symbol wrought in its iron lid. These words came to me—

'You are at the Mars Station where the Law of Action may be discovered. You stand in the Ray of Mars, in the Energy Ray. Hear me for I speak and act in the name of truth. This station marks a special point on your journey, where the source of energy for your body and soul has run dry. A new source of power is needed. There is a deep wellspring of vitality within you, but know there is no source of this energy. It is everywhere. You are living in it. My Law of Action must be followed if you wish to draw on this energy like the Woman of Samaria who came to draw water from the ancestral well. She asked, "Whence cometh this living

130

water and with what can it be drawn?" The Law provides a key. To use it and draw energy from the wellspring of life, be aware that this energy is all around and is within us. Align yourself with it, so that the energy may be converted into power, the power of action in accordance with the rhythm or flow of life. Drink from the well and let the Energy Ray pass through you.'

Further down from the well I found a spring of water that ran with the colour of blood, scarlet and magenta. The spring was well guarded with thistles and nettles and was surrounded on all sides with many types of thorn tree. Carefully, I scooped the water and drank, immediately feeling refreshed. I could feel new power coursing through my body and I had a light-headed feeling, as if now there was nothing I could not do or achieve.

The act of drinking the water was an attunement, a process of re-energising the batteries of physical power from a cosmic source. The Mars Station illumines through action the reality of spirit. And I knew that my goal was not an ideal or a dream. It was as real as the thorn that pricked my skin and drew blood, as I drank from the wellspring of life.

JUPITER

Function

Jupiter is the impulse for growth, both physical, emotional and spiritual. A key word for Jupiter is 'expansion', and with the passage of time this expansion for the human being is usually gained through the accumulation of experience. Jupiter provides the urge to explore the world, the universe, to expand the horizons of the mind beyond known limits.

Personality

Positive—Jupiter is sociable, open to ideas and devoted to the taking of opportunities. Always considering the future and what is always just beyond reach, he seeks to expand the field of consciousness by introducing new, enriching experiences. Jupiter is the philosopher, at home with abstract concepts about the nature of the universe. He is an idealistic upholder of justice and generous to a fault.

Negative—Jupiter may exhibit self-indulgence and be prone to over-exuberance. A natural social climber, he may also be snobbish, self-righteous and hypocritical. These traits mean that Jupiter may be a poor judge of the truth and may even himself exhibit lawlessness.

Mythology

Deities identified with Jupiter were: Zeus (Greek); Jupiter (Roman); Indra (Hindu); Marduk (Babylonian); Thor (Nordic); Thunor (Anglo-Saxon).

Sexual characteristics

Physically, Jupiter is large and powerful. He does not win admirers by aesthetic appeal but by force and domination. Although his experience and knowledge of the world is great, his attitude to the opposite sex is not sophisticated and is more akin to a cave-man mentality. What he cannot obtain through persuasion he will take by force.

Life cycle and crisis points

Cycle: 12 years.

Crises—Jupiter completes his cycle at 12 years old. The years 24, 36, 48, 60, 72 and 84 are all critical in terms of this cycle for they are when opportunities for growth will be won or lost.

JUPITER STATION

The little island of Iona, situated off the west coast of Scotland, has been for many years a place of pilgrimage for those who are drawn to its vital power. This place, perhaps above all, is a sacred power point, for here dwells a spirit that no one can fail to sense, an atmosphere holy and thus healing to all who visit and pay homage to the Laws that Be.

My journey took me to the small chapel of St Oran, to find there a shining silver cross and a book of wisdom lying open on the altar before it. Outside the sun shone and I was protected in this haven, surrounded by the tall, intricately carved crosses of the ancient Celtic race, whose spirit is part of every atom from which Iona is fashioned. Words from the book of wisdom began to leave the page and they danced before my eyes as I watched in wonder. These were no mere words and I shivered in awe at the mystery that they revealed.

'Fear not the unknown, for I have come to bring you gifts of wisdom. Accept these gifts with my blessing and use them well, for knowledge is not enough without the wisdom into which knowledge, like a tree, may grow. Remember that a tree cannot be forged by anything but the passage of time and you will learn that you are bound by time. Acknowledge your own growth, your own inner wisdom into which you are growing according to my Law, the Law of Jupiter, which is the Law of Unfoldment. You are the seed that contains within it the pattern of its future growth. Do not try to force this growth for you will transgress my law, but see how all that you learn grows into wisdom, how all that you experience becomes yourself. You are what you are. You are what you will always be. I am truth and wisdom and I come to you with gifts born by the Holy Ray. Step into the Ray to receive these gifts.'

And thus saying, a light of wavering purple, blue and violet hues filled the air and I was in it and it was in me. I saw a vision of an oak tree and a monk collecting strawberries in a field. And the berries turned into jewels, into amethysts and topaz.

Weariness had left me at the Mars Station and now, here in the presence of Jupiter, loneliness too. For my journey had seemed a lonely one; no-one could understand what I was about and I no longer identified myself with the cultural values of people all around me.

This isolation, of the seed from the flower, is a force that can take evolution further than cultural achievements (or flowering) of the current generation. The seed cannot return to the flower but must be an agent for future life and growth.

I realised that this was Jupiter's Law of Unfoldment, for Jupiter is concerned with future growth.

I gave thanks for the Holy Ray and was no longer alone. Down the ages many had been here before me on the Way, and now once again I could take my place among the constellations as part of a multitudinous whole. I am alive and a star among stars. Jupiter gave me the Law of Unfoldment, the Holy Ray – and a purpose.

SATURN

Function

The function of the Saturn archetype is to form structures, to define limits and to ensure that lessons are well learned. Saturn governs closely the development of the social potential of the individual, being closely associated with progress in all spheres – and its limitations. Where Jupiter seeks to move beyond limits, Saturn ensures that the individual knows where these lie. Saturn rules time and guards the borders of four-dimensional consciousness.

Personality

Positive—Saturn is a serious but profound personality, patient, reliable and organised. He exhibits self-discipline and is self-reliant. Thrift and persistence are the tools of his success, tempered even further by a sober, dutiful attitude to life.

Negative—Saturn is prone to pessimism and severe depression, brought about by rigid attitudes and a lack of human feelings. He will be mistrustful to the extent of paranoia and will exhibit a malicious streak. He can be materialistic in the extreme.

Mythology

The deities of Saturn were never the sort you would wish to meet on a dark night: Chronos (Greek); Saturn (Roman); Chiun (Babylonian); Nimb (Euphratean).

Sexual characteristics

Saturn has a morbid attraction. Secretive and sadistic, he wins friends who are usually unwilling captives and over whom he has some hold. His influence is not necessarily 'bad'; it is often simply unwanted, but irresistible nevertheless.

Life cycle and crisis points

Cycle: 29 years.

Crises—Saturn, more than any of the other planets, is associated with the lessons of life, with reaping what one has sown and experiencing the major life crises. At each return of Saturn to its position at the time of birth (29, 58 and 87 years respectively), there is a crisis point. If the problems of life have been dealt with as they occur, then all will be well, but if not, they accumulate and come back, often explosively, at each of the Saturn returns.

SATURN STATION

I knew that I was then on the very edge of being transformed, of emerging from the chrysalis in which I had so far
spent all my life. I looked around the inside of the chrysalis,
to see what form or shape its walls were now taking. I was
inside a cathedral, ornate in its architecture and powerful in
its great height and width. An organ was playing. The
complex mathematical pattern of a fugue filled the air. Now
the process must surely begin in earnest.

Suddenly all went black. Everything disappeared except
the infinite point which was my consciousness. No music,
no cathedral, no body, just a blackness. It seemed as if I had
entered a negative world, where less than nothing existed.
Then in front of me I perceived a jewel of diamond shape
that was perfect in its design and jet black in hue. I focused
on the jewel and these words came to me —

'I am the jewel of Truth. I am Saturn, Lord of Boundaries,
the Grim Reaper and Lord of Time. You shall not pass.

'Mine is the Law of Karma, of action and reaction, and it is
not until you can accept me and all the strife and suffering
that I imply that you will be released and pass through the
boundary that I guard so closely. But do not be downcast.
See here the great joy that is contained within my Saturnine
Law. I have bound you to obey the laws of nature and of
time. I have weighed you down with a physical body, with a
span of life, with work that must needs be done. When you
meet me, you meet your final limit, but, in acknowledging
that this is true, you must also see that there is a beyond, a
something more, something that lies beyond the orbit of the
Saturn Station.

'My Ray is called the Chrysalis Ray and if you step into it
you will find nothing but darkness, black, blacker than
black. Ah, but now you know that as Lord of Boundaries I
hold the key, hold a seed of light within my darkness. You
are committed to your task; you have given your word. And
remember from the ancient creed, there are three things no

man can alter: the stars in their courses, the flow of the tides, and the pattern that unrolls from the Given Word.'

My world returned and I was once more within the walls of the great cathedral, which I now recognised as Canterbury, a seat of law for the English Church. Everything was unchanged and yet different. Through Saturn, I came to realise that He is I – and that I AM. The future that lies beyond the Saturn Station will be the acknowledgement that I am He. I remembered a phrase from an ancient text: 'Behold, the earthly miracle of the caterpillar and the butterfly, of the toiling mortal and the transcendent God.' A vision of a dark forest of pine trees came to me and I knew that I had walked the path to its centre.

URANUS

Function

The psychological function of Uranus is to break down established structures. It represents sudden, unexpected change and transformation and its influence is therefore to disturb established patterns. Being also associated with the mental processes, Uranus represents inventive thought, lateral thinking and innovation. It is the astrological symbol of originality of self-expression, and of anything that deviates from the normal.

Personality

Positive—Uranus is unconventional, progressive and inventive. He may be an eccentric inventor or a radical politician. Exercising penetrative insight and a sharp intuition, Uranus is an outspoken personality who will force progress through strong argument as well as effective action.

Negative—Extreme eccentricity or even freakish abnormality may characterise Uranus. Excessive intolerance, impatience and mental aggression are all traits that can be both self-destructive and destructive towards established conventions.

Mythology

Unknown prior to its discovery in 1781, the name eventually given to this planet is that of the most ancient male deity of all, the father of Saturn. Uranus was the Greek personification of the night sky who was an offspring of the earth (Gaea). Uranus united with his mother to produce the Titans of whom one, Chronos (Saturn), removed his father's genitals with a large iron sickle.

Sexual characteristics

Uranus is the experimenter who loves to find new means of self-expression. All forms of sexual deviation are the result of the influence of Uranus.

Life cycle and crisis points

Cycle: 84 years.

Crises—Uranus brings the opportunity to change established patterns, the significant crisis points being at approximately 21, 42, 63 and 84 years. This may be a painful process if resisted, but the force of this planetary archetype is irresistible in human terms.

URANUS STATION

I am in the middle of a vicious storm of thunder and lightning and surrounded by a circle of ancient stones, the Whispering Knights and the Kingsmen of Rollright. A voice from the distant past comes to me clear as a bell, despite the roaring wind, a voice that takes me through the barrier of Saturn to the unknown that lies beyond, to the Station of Uranus.

'Meet now the Law of Transformation, as my Lightning Ray strikes deep into your heart, shattering its structure to reform once more into an organ of truth. I am Uranus, Shiva, Lord of the Burning Ground, Master of All Thresholds, Lord of Lightning and Electric Fire and, above all, Lord of Transformation. I am the breaker of static faith, the iconoclast, the challenger, ubiquitous in my role as the transformer, pitiless to those who cannot let go of past idols.

'When you move beyond the boundary of Saturn, it is I who destroys all your past beliefs and fundamental ideas with a blow as swift as lightning. When I strike, you have gone so far that there is no going back, for to be transformed is to become that which you were not and the process has no reverse. I manifest in the unexpected, for whatever you believe to lie beyond the earthly boundary of Saturn, you are wrong. I am not what you were expecting. Watch my Lightning Ray and see how my Law of Transformation has power and beauty, and destroys to build anew.'

As he spoke, I watched in my mind's eye how Uranus held up a glass prism before me. At his command a flash of silver-white lightning struck the prism and was split up by the glass to issue forth as a rainbow stream – violet, indigo, blue, green, yellow, orange and red.

Saturn having marked the end of the first stage in the process, Uranus now releases light through the personality and creates a spiritual frame of reference. The experience is of a temple within, a temple to contain the unfolding God-seed. The individual at the Uranus Station is now more than a man or woman, being a focal centre for the release of the power of the Universal Mind.

I saw a fool and knew that I had to become like him, empty-headed so that the power can enter and fill the empty space.

NEPTUNE

Function

There is an urge within the human psyche to strive towards religious experience and insight into the reality behind outward forms – an urge to seek and experience the reality of God. Neptune is the factor in operation here and is at work in the realms of the imagination and artistic or religious activity. Neptune is the planetary energy of inspiration.

Personality

Positive—Neptune is subtle and refined, lending the impression of artistic sensitivity to everything that he (or she) touches.

Negative—Gullibility is the watchword here, an easily identifiable trait of the personality in those who display religious devotion, whether to God or some other imaginative creation. Neptune can be difficult to pin down in argument. Any sort of practical activity he is involved in will immediately become confused and over-complicated.

Mythology

Neptune was associated usually with the marine deities: Poseidon (Greek); Neptune (Roman); Aegir (Nordic); Varuna (Hindu).

Sexual characteristics

Neptune embodies the mystic, and possesses the attraction of the unknown and other dimensions of reality. Drug-induced experiences are the destructive aspects of Neptune's sexual nature, while mystical visions and experiences are the positive.

140

Life cycle and crisis points

Cycle: 165 years.

Crises—Neptune affects the ideals, dreams and religious beliefs of the individual, the significant points in this cycle being 41 and 82 years. The age of 42 is also particularly significant in the Uranus cycle and this period is associated with the mid-life crisis.

NEPTUNE STATION

As I left the Uranus Station and moved again along my path, I became surrounded by a dense mist. I became totally lost in it and filled with confusion and fear of the unknown. Towering walls of an ancient ruined building seemed to loom all around me, although often I did not see them until they were right before me. From out of the mists an arm appeared, disembodied perhaps – the mists hid the body it belonged to, if indeed there was one at all. The hand held a platinum cup patterned with the trident of Neptune and containing a sea-green liquid which I knew I must drink, and although afraid to do so I downed the potion in one gulp. The drug worked fast.

'I am Neptune and I am a sea that has no form. I bring you the Law of Faith and a potion so strong that you will dissolve and become the vast ocean of life. You are no longer a drop in the ocean, you *are* the ocean. You are no longer the river, you are water flowing into the sea. Have faith and dissolve in my Mystic Ray. Give yourself to the sea.

'I am Neptune and I am a sea that has no form. I bring you the Law of Faith and a realm of ecstacy and mystic revelation. Mercy is shown in the light of true faith. Give yourself to the sea.

'I am Neptune and I am a sea that has no form. I bring you the Law of Faith and the wisdom of clairvoyance that sees to the far distant shore of infinity. I am the eye that sees all, for I am all around. Give yourself to the sea.

'Through the Law of Faith, know that you have existed and will exist for all time. Saturn bound you with time for a while, but you are beyond this now. If you look through to my eye you will see the whole future stretched before you. Look again and the past is revealed. See how these form a vast circle that meets at the point where you stand. Turn left and you will meet yourself coming from the right. Turn right and you will confront the past. Have no fear. Follow my Law of Faith, dissolve in the Mystic Ray and give yourself to the sea.'

The mist began to clear and I saw that I stood amidst the ruins of ancient Tintern Abbey. I looked at one of the great stone mandala windows, shaped in the form of petals that to me was a great orchid, high up on a wall.

Something unknown happens in the mist of Neptune, in the 'cloud of unknowing'. A transfiguration takes place and out of it emerges the mystic, in full awareness of the whole process. The abbey became then a huge structure of coral, formed from the activity of life both microscopic and macroscopic, and on this coral structure played a soft light of lavender and mauve that turned into a milky whiteness. The white colour reveals to the enlightened eye innocence, holiness and simplicity, radiant as the moon, beautiful as the dawn. So now the divine virginity of life shines forth free from tincture, and with no blemish.

PLUTO

Function

Pluto is the principle of rebirth. Often associations are made with the process of death, but this is only half of Pluto's action, the other half being birth. Pluto rules the mysteries of birth and death, of beginnings and ends, on whatever level is appropriate. Pluto will bring into consciousness hidden complexes or problems, and these revelations cannot be ignored. This process usually either transforms or destroys.

Personality

The positive and negative qualities of the Pluto personality are indivisible, being those of the power to renew, rejuvenate or resurrect that which has died or become petrified. Pluto in psychological terminology represents aspects of the Shadow, the sum total of all our negative personality traits which, if denied, can destroy, but if recognised and integrated can become a source of renewal.

Mythology

In classical mythology Pluto ruled the underworld (equals the unconscious). To the Greeks, Hades (Pluto) was the ruler of the realms of the dead, together with his wife Persephone. He is also known, however, as the giver of wealth, ruling 'buried treasure'.

Sexual characteristics

Pluto is concerned directly with the sexual act and seeks gratification of the urge to release pent-up feelings and tension. Keen to generate sexual excitement, Pluto is single-minded, with little concern for matters of love and the emotions. His aim is to capture and rule and once caught it is difficult to escape from him.

Life cycle and crisis points

Cycle: 248 years.

Crises—Pluto, as mentioned, effects the crises of self-transformation through the eruption of unconscious processes and influences. The main crisis point is at 62 years of age.

PLUTO STATION

The journey is approaching its climax, as I walk slowly and reverently with others in a procession that moves through Avebury, from the heights of Silbury Hill to the mighty West Kennet long barrow, where the seed of the summer crop is to be put into storage. It is to be placed in the cervix of the Earth Mother's womb, there to lie throughout the barren winter months, and await its germination in the spring. To all intents and purposes, the seed is dead.

I lead the funeral procession, and as I enter the portal of the great long barrow the earth opens beneath my feet and I sink down into the realm that lies below the earth, a realm inhabited by the dead and ruled by Pluto. I have arrived at the Pluto Station, the last known lamp that lights the way of travellers. And there stands Pluto before me. I look into his glowing red eyes and know that I am facing death. The red of Pluto's eyes set me on fire and yet the redness of the fire cannot be that which flames in fury or smoulders in passion, for it is the unchanging fire that illumines but does not consume, the fire of radiant spiritual love. And Pluto guides me through his realm, speaking thus —

'Three things hold the Secret of Life – the corn in the earth, the child in the womb and the dream at the heart of the minstrel's song.

'Mine is the Law of Immortality and to follow my Law you must first descend to the depths, following my Ray of Death. At my station you have become the cosmic seed and that contains the Magic Pattern. The seed must descend to the depths for "three days in Hell".

'Deep in my realm lies a buried treasure, infinite riches beyond the puny dreams of man. They are yours if you will follow my Law. And this Law, the greatest of all, teaches how life follows death, how death must precede life, how the two are one. Each time you learn, each time you reach a new part in the process, a new planetary station, a part of you dies. You are never the same again. The past dies as

144

each future moment is born in the present. Travel my Ray of Death and discover the Law of Immortality. Be judged by the final ordeal of temptation. But turn away now from my eyes of death and all is lost.'

I must die. Before me is the vision of a red stone, burning with a fire that does not consume, while in and around the flames dance words from the Book of Wisdom: 'He that believeth in me, though he were dead, yet shall he live.'

When we face death, Pluto guards the path that leads us through unconscious death – or crucifixion – away from the solar system and into the infinite empty space between the stars, only we now find that we are heading, inevitably, miraculously, joyfully, straight into the heart of the sun, for the final cosmic integration.

THE SUN

Function

The sun represents the process of self-integration, or 'individuation', whereby a person becomes whole and fulfilled. It symbolises the life force and therefore the true Self, the centre of personality. It is a masculine, outpouring force, which astrologers interpret as having the greatest influence on the growth of the personal ego. The sun can be seen as representing the ultimate purpose of the individual's life – the search for and discovery of the Self.

Personality

Positive—The sun is ambitious, with an urge for power. He is a leader, a creative person whose aim is self-reliance and individuality. His actions are all purposeful.

Negative—A self-centred and egotistical personality, the sun can be aggressive and destructive. He can display a boastful nature that seeks to dominate, but which demonstrates incompetence.

Mythology

The sun gods of all mythologies give insights into the character of the sun such as: Adonis, Apollo, Helios (Greek); Ammon, Horus, Ra, Osiris (Egyptian); Sol (Roman); Balder (Nordic); Quetzalcoatl (Aztec); Vishnu (Indian); Dazhbog (Slavonic); Shamash (Sumero-Akkadian).

Sexual characteristics

The sun is a virile, masculine energy, epitomised by the sun gods of Greek mythology. Expressing physical beauty and perfection, the sun inspires mortals who appreciate this beauty, but cannot attain it for themselves.

Life cycle and crisis points

Cycle: 365¼ days.

Crises—The birthday period indicates a time when there may be a need to slow down as physical energy could be low. There are three other alleged low-vitality periods of the year associated with the solar cycle, at three-monthly intervals from the birth date. Simply note when energy highs and lows occur during the year and make adjustments to compensate for these changes in energy flow.

SUN STATION

Within the stone circle I watch the marriage of the sun with the moon, when white becomes silver and red becomes gold, after the eclipse of death. This marks the beginning and the end. Stonehenge marks the final power point, the Sun Station whose circle marks the perimeter of the temenos or protected sacred ground wherein is enacted the rite of integration, individuation or enlightenment – a secret and sacred rite of which we know nothing and yet, if we can face

146

death consciously, of which we can know everything. The cycle is complete and we are witnessing at long last the Law of One, the matrimony of heaven and earth, of the male and the female, so that the whole of creation may be revealed in all its glory. The Law of One rides on a Golden Ray and whoever is bathed in this Ray shall realise the Holy Mystical Marriage and be One with the Self. When the Self is realised collectively, there can be no king where every man is king, no queen where every woman is queen, by divine right.

Now is the stone shaped, the elixir of life prepared, the love-child or child of love born, the new birth completed and the work made whole or perfect. This is the Child of the Virgin, her first born, this is the noble hero, the redeemer of the serpent, who transforms the dragon. For now the Child of Paradise is become clear as transparent glass, in which the Divine Sun shines through and through, like gold that is wholly bright, pure and clear, and from henceforth the Divine Child is in thine own nature become one with God.

CHAPTER 8

FROM CRISIS TO GROWTH

One aim of the exploration of inner space is to break out of the continuous repetition of the same behaviour patterns and to discover our life cycles. These should-form a background foundation for the development of maturity. This final chapter summarises the practical approach for achieving this aim.

Is there any direct relationship between the cosmos and the human individual? This question must be divided into two parts. In terms of simple cause and effect the answer is yes. The sun, for example, influences life on earth to such a degree that we are dependent on it; without it life could not exist at all. However, the second part to this question is an astrological one. Do the positions of the stars and planets and the relationships between them determine, or even affect, the personality and life of the individual?

Again considering cause and effect and external influence, the answer is no. For example, it has been described how the constellations[1] did not exist before human beings gave them their patterns and significance (pages 29–30). There are numerous other examples of this lack of physical connection. For example, one of the methods that astrologers use for predictive purposes equates the movement of a planet over the course of one day with the life of an individ-

---

1.   It is notable that the word 'constellation' in analytical psychology refers to a group of ideas felt to be related, giving the immediate connotation that the starry constellations are a product of the mind.

ual over the course of one year. The method is symbolic and does not relate to the actual positions of the planets at a particular point in time of the individual's life.

Astrological influences do not come from outside us – they stem from within, from the unconscious realms of the human psyche, from inner, not outer space. In this context, the question is not the right one because we are being influenced by ourselves.

This then begs the question 'What is the self?' We would normally define its boundary as being that of the physical body, but modern physics tells us now that boundaries are an illusion, objects or things are an illusion, only relationships exist (see pages 22–3). Asking a question such as 'Do the planets influence us?' implies that there is an object (the planet) and a subject (our selves). This hidden implication must be removed with the realisation that the subject and object cannot be separated. They do not exist independently but in relationship with one another. They exist *because* they are related and one would not exist without the other.

From this point of view, the world is full of paradoxes. Such questions as the ones I have posed cannot be answered either 'yes' or 'no'. The paradoxical answer is 'yes *and* no', which is not a cop out but a way of saying that the answer depends on which way you look at the problem. We thus create our own reality.

To understand fully the meaning of this statement and its consequences, the answers lie within. The journey through inner space, with its subsequent discoveries, is a psychological route to taking responsibility for the realities of life.

We have seen that the exploration of inner space and the development of new forms of consciousness can be achieved by using astrology as a guide or map. Its symbols graphically depict the processes at work in the unconscious. These and the cycles and patterns which these processes entail have been described in the foregoing chapters. It now only remains to tie all this detail together so that inner experiences can be used for practical benefit.

The visualisation method of guided imagery introduced in Chapter 2 and given substance through subsequent descriptions can be used in any of a number of ways, depending on the choice of the individual. This may be to gain material effects, secure fulfilling relationships or success in one's chosen career, or for the more abstract purposes of self-development, self-fulfilment and the expansion of consciousness; the technique can be adapted and developed appropriately.

Inner work of this kind is never enough, however, as we all have to live in the world of everyday existence, coping with the stresses of daily life. To bring the discoveries of inner space through into this mundane reality it is necessary to take some active steps. One important task will be to keep a personal diary. This should detail both dreams and the results of inner work and meditations. The process of describing these often stimulates the memory so that further details are recalled and their meanings become clear.

It is not just the individual occurrences and circumstances of inner experiences that are important but the pattern of their unfolding development with the passage of time. The same is true for the events that take place in the outer, material world. A diary of inner experiences kept together with a description of personal outer circumstances and events will, in time, reveal the holistic relationship between inner and outer realities and prove beyond doubt how 'chance' occurrences have a deliberate cause that lies in the unconscious.

If this suggestion is accepted, it can then lead to a positive method for dealing with personal problems and crises which, although they may take on the appearance of being thrust upon the individual by external events beyond his or her control, are discovered to be deceptions, whereby the real cause lies within, albeit on an unconscious level. Inner exploration then provides the means for bringing these unconscious elements into the light of day. In doing this, a remarkable reversal of fortunes can be achieved, for a situation that may have been negative, destructive, frought with difficulty, even a crisis of seemingly unsolvable proportions, will give way to become a quantum leap in consciousness that is positive and creative. Problems will have no power to rule the individual who has thus conformed with the will of nature, and made what was unconscious and an inhabitant of the dark underworlds come into the light of day.

The alchemists expressed this process as a sacred marriage, the formation of a relationship between opposites. In following the path that I have described, there may initially be an understandable fear that the marriage between spirit and matter cannot take place without some sort of loss. This fear is that the conscious self, the ego, may be absorbed irretrievably into the darkness of the unconscious. But this will not be so, for the effect of the marriage is to retain the individuality of the constituent parts, but with a holistic relationship formed between them. In material terms, the outer world no longer appears completely fated and beyond comprehension but takes on a new aura as life is breathed into it. From this point of view, nothing is disconnected, or beyond our responsibility and need for caring; everything has an inner life of its own, from the physical being of our biological functions to the hardest crystal.

If it is remembered that the unconscious can be defined as what we don't recognise as part of our selves, then it becomes possible to conceive that planetary cycles, the physical body, and indeed all matter, really are interrelated and have an influence on human behaviour and growth. However, as we have seen, this is not so simply in terms of cause and effect. Moreover, it illustrates the point that it is necessary to reconcile this view of interconnectedness of inner and outer space with the materialistic, mechanistic view of reality which alienates and cuts off the individual from his or her environment. Our symbols of meaning and purpose will then be reinvested with their power to transform, enlighten and make whole, and thus release once more the power of the gods as formative principles in the true process of creation.

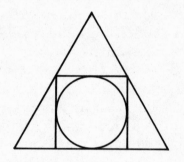

SUGGESTED ADDITIONAL READING

Arroyo, Stephen, *Astrology, Psychology and the Four Elements*, CRCS, 1975

Bennett, J.G., *Deeper Man*, Aquarian Press, 1985

Bohm, David, *Wholeness and the Implicate Order*, Ark, 1980

Campbell, Joseph, *The Masks of God* (Four Volumes), Penguin, 1962

Capra, Fritjov, *The Tao of Physics*, Fontana, 1983

Cooper, J.C., *An Illustrated Encyclopaedia of Traditional Symbols*, Thames & Hudson, 1978

Dossey, L., *Space, Time and Medicine*, Shambhala, 1982

Ferrucci, Piero, *What We May Be*, Aquarian Press, 1982

Eliade, Mircea, *Myths, Dreams & Mysteries*, Harvill Press, 1960

Ferguson, Marilyn, *The Aquarian Conspiracy*, Granada, 1982

Gilchrist, Cherry, *Alchemy – The Great Work*, Aquarian Press, 1984

Greene, Liz, *Relating*, Coventure, 1977

Harding, M. Esther, *Woman's Mysteries, Ancient and Modern*, Rider, 1971

Hawking, Stephen W., *A Brief History of Time*, Bantam, 1988

Jung, C.G., *Dreams* (from *The Collected Works*), Bollingen Series, 1974

Jung, C.G., *Memories, Dreams, Reflections*, Fontana, 1967

Jung, C.G., *Modern Man in Search of a Soul*, Routledge & Kegan Paul, 1961

Jung, C.G., *Synchronicity*, Routledge & Kegan Paul, 1972

Lievegoed, Bernard, *Phases*, Rudolf Steiner Press, 1982

Lundsted, Betty, *Planetary Cycles*, Weiser, 1984

Mattoon, M.A., *Applied Dream Analysis*, Wiley & Sons, 1978

Mayo, Jeff, *The Planets and Human Behaviour*, Fowler, 1972

Milner, Dennis, *Explorations of Consciousness*, Spearman, 1978

Oken, Alan, *Alan Oken's Complete Astrology*, Bantam, 1988

Ouspensky, P.D., *A New Model of the Universe*, Routledge & Kegan Paul, 1974

Page, James Lynn, *Applied Visualisation*, Quantum, 1990

Peto, Les, *The Dream Lover*, Quantum, 1990

Rudhyar, Dane, *Astrology and the Modern Psyche*, CRCS, 1976

Rudhyar, Dane, *The Lunation Cycle*, Aurora, 1986

Rudhyar, Dane, *The Pulse of Life*, Shambala, 1970

Ruperti, Alexander, *Cycles of Becoming*, CRCS, 1978

Steinbrecher, Edwin C., *The Inner Guide Meditation*, Aquarian Press, 1988

Swainson, Mary & Bennett, Louisa, *Psychic Sense*, Quantum, 1990

Tart, Charles T., *Altered States of Consciousness*, Doubleday Anchor, 1972

Von Franz, M.-L., *Alchemical Active Imagination*, Spring Publications, 1979

Von Franz, M.-L., *On Divination and Synchronicity*, Inner City Books, 1980

Von Franz, M.-L. & Hillman, James, *Jung's Typology*, Spring Publications, 1971

Wilson, Colin, *The New Existentialism*, Wildwood House, 1980

Wolf, Fred Alan, *Taking The Quantum Leap*, Harper & Row, 1989

Zohar, Danah, *The Quantum Self*, Bloomsbury, 1990

INDEX

quadruplicities, the, 63
qualities, the, 64
quantum theory, 22–4

reality, nature of, 20–1, 37
rebirths
  in the life cycle, 102
relationships, human, 32
relaxation exercises, 47–8
repression, 36, 44
Rudhyar, Dane, 19

Sagittarius, 101, 108–9
Saturn, 110, 134–7
science, 21–2
Scorpio, 100, 107–8, 116
seasons, cycle of the, 106–17
self-knowledge, 20
signs, 18
signs of the zodiac, see zodiac,
  signs of the
spring, 110–12
square, as a symbol, 76
stages of life, 93–104
  polar opposites in the, 103
Steinbrecher, Edwin C., 59
Steiner, Rudolf, 74
subconscious, see unconscious
summer, 112–14
sun, 145–7
superstition, 31
symbols, 18
  archetypal and personal
    meaning of, 35–6
  astrological, see astrological
    symbols; planets; zodiac,
    signs of the

personality and interpretation
  of, 42–3
personified, 56
polarity of, 70
synchronicity, 24, 39

Taoism, 25
Taurus, 95, 112–13
technology, 20
third force, 73–4
time, 21
triangle of forces, 73
triplicities, the, 63
types, psychological, 76–9

unconscious, 28, 44
  collective, 44
universe
  theory of creation of the, 80–1
Uranus, 93, 137–9

Venus, 113, 116, 127–8
Virgo, 98, 115
Vulcan, 116

Watts, Alan, 25
winter, 107–10
Wolf, Fred Alan, 22

zodiac, 62–3
zodiac, signs of the, 105–7
  and archetypal energies, 75
  feminine and masculine
    qualities of, 70–3
  keywords and, 63, 69
  see also names of individual
    signs, e.g. Aries